OTHER GROUNDS

Before you start to read this book, take this moment to think about making a donation to punctum books, an independent non-profit press,

@ https://punctumbooks.com/support/

If you're reading the e-book, you can click on the image below to go directly to our donations site. Any amount, no matter the size, is appreciated and will help us to keep our ship of fools afloat. Contributions from dedicated readers will also help us to keep our commons open and to cultivate new work that can't find a welcoming port elsewhere. Our adventure is not possible without your support.
Vive la open-access.

Fig. 1. Hieronymus Bosch, *Ship of Fools* (1490–1500)

OTHER GROUNDS: BREAKING FREE OF THE CORRELATIONIST CIRCLE. Copyright © 2016 David Lindsay. This work carries a Creative Commons BY-NC-SA 4.0 International license, which means that you are free to copy and redistribute the material in any medium or format, and you may also remix, transform, and build upon the material, as long as you clearly attribute the work to the authors and editors (but not in a way that suggests the authors or punctum books endorses you and your work), you do not use this work for commercial gain in any form whatsoever, and that for any remixing and transformation, you distribute your rebuild under the same license. http://creativecommons.org/licenses/by-nc-sa/4.0/

First published in 2016 by punctum books, Earth, Milky Way.
www.punctumbooks.com

ISBN-13: 978-0692715185
ISBN-10: 0692715185
Library of Congress Cataloging Data is available from the Library of Congress

Book design: Natalia Tuero German & Vincent W.J. van Gerven Oei
Cover image: Adaptation of Ralph Crane, "A cat being dropped upside down to demonstrate how a cat's movements while falling can be imitated by astronauts in space," 1968. Source: LIFE Photo Archive, hosted by Google.

OTHER GROUNDS

BREAKING FREE OF THE CORRELATIONIST CIRCLE

David Lindsay

Is there any possibility of a fresh and concrete research into the secret contours of objects?
—Graham Harman, *Towards Speculative Realism* (2010)

I would venture to suggest that even the meagre amount of knowledge of the use of the self contained in these pages may be sufficient to enable workers in all fields of investigation, whether in biology, astronomy, physics, philosophy, psychology, or any other, to realize that in their researches they have passed over a field of experience which, if explored, would add new material to the premises from which to make their several deductions.
—F.M. Alexander, *The Use of the Self* (1946)

Contents

Introduction · You're on the List! (Oh, Wait—)
11

1 · Here Comes Two of You
17

2 · A Real Class Act
35

3 · Stalking the Wild Implicit Mind
67

4 · Personal Effects
95

5 · Public Things
119

Acknowledgments · The Means Whereby a Book…
149

Appendix · Greater Than Zero, Less Than Everything
153

Bibliography
155

INTRODUCTION

You're on the List! (Oh, Wait —)

Roses, laser beams, Jupiter, humans, elbow noodles…

The philosophical movement known as object-oriented ontology, or OOO, has produced many lists like the one above — so many, in fact, that they've earned the nickname of Latour litanies,[1] after Bruno Latour, who first made them popular. They're certainly fun to write. Think of an object, then a second object with no obvious relation to the first, then a third that breaks the pattern again. Continue as desired, and the world is quickly revealed to be vast and dense with beings of mind-boggling variety.

So what is this movement, with its name that evokes computer programming jargon in one moment and erotic novels the next, and what's the point of making these lists?

After netting out the usual internecine disputes, the point of departure for all object-oriented ontologists, along with their cousins the speculative realists, is a rejection of correlationism. As coined by Quentin Meillassoux, correlationism is the assertion that thinking and being can never be considered separately from one another. The milder version of correlationism might be stated: What lies beyond thought can't be known, but it can be imagined. The stronger version offers less wiggle room. What lies beyond thought, it claims, can't even be considered without triggering a contradiction. The correlationist view is generally seen to trace back at least to Kant, gathering steam with Heidegger's notion of concealment, and reaching its apogee in

---

1 Credit for this term is due to Ian Bogost.

postmodernism, with its heavy-lidded insistence on the world as a text.

OOO rejects correlationism in any of its guises, and offers an alternative. It concedes that all objects retain some aspect that is unreachable. I can experience a cup in many ways, but there will always be some part of the cup that remains *withdrawn* from me. Following from this — and here is the key move — it maintains that objects remain withdrawn from each other as well. Therefore, we *do* know something about that which lies beyond thought, and what we know usurps us from our presumptive central position in the universe. OOO decenters the human and alerts us to a "concealed underworld of real objects" (Graham Harman), a "mesh" (Tim Morton), or a "wilderness" (Levi Bryant), in which all objects enjoy equal footing, or what some have called a flat ontology. Such is the impetus behind the litanies: the challenge that each of the objects you name has equal status as a thing that actually exists. A bear exists, as does a spelling bee, as does a toaster.

This argument has the force of logic behind it and — though it makes my job harder to say it — the folly of life in front. The problem shows up with the fourth item on my list, which both belongs and does not belong with the others, is both included and excluded, because it includes myself… and the list came from *me*. While drawing attention to this paradox might seem fussy, since the name of my species on a page and my actual self are pretty clearly two different things, I believe it presents a serious difficulty for anyone interested in the nature of being, *especially* those of us who aim to make good on claims of decentering the human. What can it mean, after all, to regard all objects as equal, if we're the ones doing the regarding? Doesn't that already grant us a special place in our scheme? How exactly do you remain faithful to the principle of decentering the human if not from some central human position? Conversely, on what basis can we hope to judge our success in understanding that which, by our own admission, is inexorably foreign to us? As one critic puts it in reviewing a book by vitalist Jane Bennett:

Towards the end of *Vibrant Matter,* its author asks: "…what if we loosened the tie between participation and human language use, encountering the world as a swarm of vibrant materials entering and leaving agentic assemblages?" In failing to suggest both why and how our current societies could feasibly encounter the world on this way, *Vibrant Matter* inadvertently raises some critical questions about the epistemic community to which its author belongs.[2]

Such questions aren't easily waved away. The prevailing defense, advanced in different forms by Harman and Bryant, is to hold that all objects distort their relations with other objects, just as we humans do. If this is the case, then we are equal to other objects, and equally correlationist. *Every* object caricatures other objects, so the equality is complete.

The "decentering of the correlation" argument has the virtue of consistency, and it opens important lines of inquiry. The difficulty I have is that it seems to run past its own best idea. If we distort or caricature other objects, then we will be distorting other objects when we speak of how they distort each other, so it will be true once again that we can't know being outside ourselves. We can agree that other objects exist independently of us, but past that we reach a discursive dead end. This looks very much like where Kant ended up when he declared the thing-in-itself off limits, and very much, too, as if we are destined to color every litany with our own, all-too-human perspective. At the very least, it undermines the rejection of correlationism that's supposed to form the cornerstone of the ooo project.

Perhaps it's possible, as Bryant has it, that attempts at empathy will help us to understand how other objects experience the world, so long as we remember that we are distorting them. Perhaps there's something to be gained from the embrace of caricature. Perhaps the growing interest in an object-oriented aesthetics, and in metaphor, has merit in its own right. For my

---

2 Noel Castree, review of *Vibrant Matter* by Jane Bennett, http://societyandspace.com/?s=Jane++Bennett (accessed November 8, 2014).

part, I think there actually is a way out. On this count, I side with Meillassoux in taking correlationism to be a worthy adversary — worthy, that is, of both respect and ruin.

In the following pages, then, it will be my aim to resolve the contradiction triggered by our participation in the roster of being, and in so doing, to open a path that I believe has hitherto been overlooked: the possibility of decentering the human beyond mere assertion. My argument will hinge on a subtle distinction in the concept of independence. While I will do my best to defend the theoretical independence of objects from thought, the pay dirt will come if I can show independence as a variety of experience.

This emphasis on experience will entail a turn toward practice, although possibly not in the usual sense of the word. One often sees this term hitched to what turns out to be another idea: to incorporate a theory into a plan, so to speak. I mean it in a different sense — as when someone learns a passage on a violin. An object-oriented practice for me is iterative, and it vanishes, just like music does. It can be learned, but never finished, precisely because it is the practice of a thought, rather than a final resting place for it.

For reasons that will become clear, a practice of this kind will not have much to do with the internecine disputes I've mentioned. The field has become varied enough, however, that one must distinguish the version of ooo to which one subscribes, and to take in tow views that lie outside it as well. I've already mentioned Meillassoux, who doesn't consider himself an object-oriented ontologist at all. His book, *After Finitude*, was the wake-up call for me, as it has been for many others. Although he may disagree with my thesis, I also recognize a kindred spirit in Levi Bryant,[3] partly for his perennial disposition toward "getting something going," and often for the specific arguments he

---

3 Bryant has recently moved away from the term "object" in favor of the more dynamic "machine." Insofar as this choice is meant to emphasize the functionality of an object in addition to its state, I will take the preference to be largely a matter of definition and retain the more widely used "object."

has to make. In a kind of severe shorthand, I would point to his Ontic Principle: "There is no difference that does not make a difference."[4] In other words, the identity of objects can be known by the differences they generate. I hold that it's possible to formalize this principle in such a way as to bring out the existence of another being without "overwriting" it. Given that I can't know the totality of another object, I still can change my relation to it and so gain some knowledge about it. More to the point, I can make a change that allows *another* change to come from *another* place. That these changes can be brought about through the construction of objects (or the construction of relations to objects) is also important to my argument, and those familiar with the writings of Ian Bogost will recognize my debt to him on this count.[5]

In thinking along these lines, I'm consciously taking up a second-phase position. OOO rightly began by emphasizing the reality of objects other than the human, in order to make a new thesis clear. The original stirring salvoes have since given way to more nuanced expositions, in which correlationist views are sometimes granted validity as realities in their own right (since correlationisms are objects too). But these redactions often have an air of haste about them, as when the city dweller praises the local museums and opera houses she will never visit. What remains to be done, here in the second phase, is to look long and hard at the human object, and to see if we might resolve our status in the litanies, based on the kind of things we are.

My opening, then, will engage Bryant's view as set forth in *The Democracy of Objects,* in order to reveal a surprising and weird relation *within* the human object — the apparent existence of two minds in a single body. In Chapter Two, I resolve some

---

4   Levi R. Bryant. "The Ontic Principle: Outline of an Object-Oriented Ontology," in *The Speculative Turn: Materialism and Realism,* ed. Levi Bryant, Nick Srnicek, and Graham Harman (Melbourne: re:press, 2011), 264.

5   As my argument proceeds, the reader will no doubt hear the echoes of voices that have come before me. I apologize in advance for not mentioning them all. My only excuse is that I have tried to follow the logical consequences of a premise, and to be content with allies after the fact.

ambiguities in the argument for coincident entities by casting both their normal operations and the possibility of decentering those operations in mathematical terms. That accomplished, I turn in Chapter Three to an existing method for decentering our coincident entities and, after reconciling it with my mathematical forays, identify its ethical limitations when it comes to the production of artifacts. Chapter Four is then taken up with the work of recasting colocation in terms of intention, so as to clear the way for Chapter Five, a more freewheeling section in which I break protocol and advance specific proposals for practicing an object-oriented ethics.

The dreaded word mathematics, sitting right there in my summary, is bound to set off alarms. My hope is that any fears of an impenetrable text will prove unfounded. Certainly, I'm not a schooled mathematician, but rather self-taught in almost every respect. The same goes for my philosophical training, which more closely resembles the accumulations of a medieval wandering scholar than it does the progressive conquest of degrees. My promise, then, is to advance no concept that I haven't unraveled on my own (sometimes, admittedly, after considerable mental exertion). Show your work, the teachers say, and I have tried to do so, not only because philosophy has become increasingly compartmentalized, resulting in a profusion of different terms for similar ideas, but also because the greater project of existence, as I understand it, belongs to all of us. Again practice is the operative term, and the leveler of every good theory: After all the arguments and objections, the defeat of correlationism begins at home.

1

Here Comes Two of You

In the movie *Toy Story*, there's a scene in which Buzz Lightyear sees a commercial about an action-figure astronaut who walks, talks, and looks unaccountably like him, and even bears his name. Having strenuously denied up to this point that he's a toy, Buzz is suddenly struck mute. It seems impossible, yet there it is. The viewer might be forgiven for identifying with him in his puzzlement, since we are made of stuff, too. How can I be thinking if I am this thing? Am I, in fact, this thing, even though I can't fathom how it could be so?

My aim in this book will be to reconcile the strangeness of being a thinking object, and therefore somehow different from other objects, with the possibly even stranger idea of being an object on par with other things, and so in some way equal to everything else. The assertion of equality, a cornerstone of object-oriented ontology, is almost trivial to demonstrate in theory. A pear tree exists just as truly as does a typewriter, just as truly as does a civil war or a black hole, and the same can easily be said for a human being without further delay. But in order to render this position practical — to actually *do* something on an equal footing with other objects — it seems evident that one must begin with the object one is, and this is not so simple.

As with our action-figure hero, we usually don't think of ourselves as objects. In fact, it's difficult to maintain this line of thought when presented with the evidence. If we try to separate our thoughts from our own existence, from our own nuts and bolts, we're essentially trying, as the skeptic David Hume put it, to catch ourselves without having a perception,[1] and the attempt to make sense of such a pursuit has proven discouraging, even for those who make it their business. My entry into the fray will involve isolating an entity that, strange as it sounds, actually shares my hardware with me, and then capitalizing on the difference between this other entity and me, in order to resolve the vexing circularity of trying to "find oneself." The core idea of this procedure is not original with me. My contribution, such as it stands, will be to extract its basic structure, so as to be able to apply it to my relations to other objects — those pear trees and typewriters, and then some.

Of course, for some, my insistence on describing humans as objects will be typical of everything that's wrong with society. To objectify humans is, after all, to make them ends to be gained, and so to encourage various forms of aggressive behavior or materialistic consumption, or to strengthen the complicit link between them. The complaint is understandable, given the hostilities crowding the horizon, but, to be annoyingly correct, it confuses the claims that object-oriented ontology actually makes. If proponents of ooo rarely use the term *subject*, it's largely because they're *oriented* toward objects, which is not the same thing as denying the existence of subjects. On the contrary, it's possible to push the argument until all objects do something resembling thinking. For the object-oriented, the assertion of thingness is not reductive of humans so much as it is generous to the inanimate.

So much sounds gracious enough, yet having granted that everything exists, I may still insist on a residue of uniqueness. Am I not special merely by virtue of my ability to entertain these considerations? Certainly. I readily concede the uniqueness of the human position. But I also concede the uniqueness of a waterfall. The question is: What propels us to think of other be-

---

[1] "For my part, when I enter most intimately into what I call myself, I always stumble on some particular perception or other, of heat or cold, light or shade, love or hatred, pain or pleasure. I never can catch myself at any time without a perception, and never can observe anything but the perception." David Hume, *A Treatise of Human Nature* (New York: Barnes & Noble, 2005), 194.

ings — waterfalls and all the rest — as extensions of our agenda at the cost of the equal information they provide, and what might be attempted from within our special disposition, whatever it turns out to be, that could open a communication line for receiving that information?

In addressing these questions, I will take the account provided by Levi Bryant in his book, *The Democracy of Objects,* as my point of departure.

On Bryant's view, which he has christened *onticology,* every being is made up of two parts: its *local manifestation* — how it appears at any given time — and its *virtual proper being* — the withdrawn remainder that is never exhausted by its local manifestations. This will hold for panthers and for paperweights, and it will hold for humans. As a local manifestation, a human might have lots of hair at one age and none at another, be small in youth and tall in middle age, and charming at unreliable intervals. Throughout these changes, there will be some *power* to manifest that never appears — its virtual proper being.[2]

Most people will easily point to examples of locally manifested humans and, if pressed, will also admit to a certain ineffability in them that could qualify as a virtual being. This virtuality seems to add a wrinkle, though, because we are, to all accounts, *in* it. Normally, object-oriented ontologists establish the withdrawal of objects and promptly move on to implications. My challenge is different, because the best candidate for the human's virtual being is agency, or thought itself, and after all the strivings of philosophy, agency has turned out to be a fairly cold case. In *Consciousness Explained,* Daniel Dennett poses the difficulty vividly: In order to explain an observation that takes place in the brain, it seems necessary for there to be some kind of interior space, or Cartesian Theater, in which the observation can take place.[3] But if this is so, then we surely ought to be able to find it, and no one has succeeded so far. While we can patently affirm

---

2 Levi Bryant, *The Democracy of Objects* (Ann Arbor: Open Humanities Press, 2011), 69.
3 Daniel C. Dennett, *Consciousness Explained* (Boston: Little, Brown and Company, 1991), 104–11.

that thinking takes place (at least sometimes!), the actual location of our mental activity remains elusive.

The question as to whether or not thoughts occupy space is a good one, and I will take it up later in these pages. For the moment, what Bryant's onticology allows us to hazard is that the human object is simply the human body, because this will immediately mean that there is something in the human body that gives us the same chase that we encounter whenever we try to locate a mind. Far from being troubled by the terrible attendance record for the executive director of our being, we should *expect* there to be infinite regress. If we look at a being we recognize as a human, we can simply take for granted that there is something about this human that will necessarily evade our every scrutiny.

All objects withdraw. The mind is withdrawn from the human body. Therefore, the mind is the virtual being of the human object. We don't know for certain that this deduction is true, but the reasoning is sound enough for the sake of argument.

Continuing with Bryant's onticological line of reasoning, then, I will also maintain that the mind is real. The withdrawn portion of an object is held to be really there. It's not said to be non-existent simply by virtue of its withdrawal. This doesn't force me into an extreme position, since I can just as easily assert the reality of gravity as the virtual being of a planet without being able to find anything but its effects. We do not hold gravity to be unreal — at least not on these grounds. Withdrawal is the norm throughout the universe, not the exception.

So thought is what recedes from the human object — problem solved? Not exactly. Onticology, along with most other arguments about the composition of objects, allows us to consider the body as a part of other objects — in Bryant's terms, its exo-relations. Even if it is subsumed into another object, such as a family or a society, the human object will resist totalization. So much seems eminently plausible. There will always be some aspect of "me" that escapes my family or the society in which I live.

A disturbance appears, however, when we consider the human object's endo-relations — the objects that the human contains.[4]

As a matter of consistency, the objects within the body will resist totalization just as the body frustrates totalization by objects without. I won't know everything there is to know about my heart. This is useful, because for the heart to operate without my intervention eliminates a great deal of micro-managing! Notice too, though, that there are two withdrawals in play, one from the heart and another from the entire body inside which the heart resides, neither of which be referenced as my *own* awareness. The example is not arbitrary. On his website, *Larval Subjects,* Bryant addresses the problem of endo-relations by referring to cells as objects within the human object, and one can see what motivates his choice.[5] It's quite amazing to contemplate the comings and goings of cells while the organism endures. The stakes are low in his example, however, because while cells are undoubtedly objects, their very expendability implies that they make no difference to the body. The heart makes a significant difference, because the body cannot continue without it. Of course, where many cells expire at once, they will make an evident difference, but this is also precisely where the body's existence independent of them is thrown into jeopardy.

The point isn't overturned by the transience of cells making up the heart. Whatever is crucial to the function that the heart serves — be it an artificial pump or a gene sequence — is tantamount to the part on which the body is dependent. Yet the human body is not entirely manifested as the heart.

Here a doubt arises: Doesn't this interdependence of local manifestations simply confirm the mortality of their corresponding virtual beings? In one sense, yes — separate the parts and agency disappears. On the other hand, something occurred to make their interdependence endure, yet I'm hard put to identify myself as the cause of this endurance. Descartes makes this

[4] Bryant, *The Democracy of Objects,* 68.
[5] Levi Bryant, "Three: Strange Mereologies," *Larval Subjects*, May 1, 2010, http://larvalsubjects.wordpress.com/2010/05/01/three-strange-mereologies/ (accessed June 30, 2014).

precise point an important link in his ontological argument for the existence of God. "It does not follow that because I existed a little earlier, I must exist now, unless at this moment some cause produces and creates me a new, so to speak, that is to say, conserves me."[6]

There are many ways to take down Descartes' ontological argument, yet whatever rebuttal we choose, this part of his case remains formidable. Even if we rule out that the interdependence of heart and body was intended in advance, the persistence of their interdependence *as such* requires the admission of a virtual being that organizes the parts of the body without my conscious involvement. Grant that the interdependence is contingent and the point still holds. Something favors the interdependence of heart and body over their independence — *for as long as it does*.

Now we can take the argument home. Once the heart is admitted as a necessary part of the body, it's trivial to ask whether the *brain* also entails a withdrawal from the body that is different from thought. If so, there will be two virtual beings that we recognize as overall coordinators of the same local manifestation. That is, if the non-brain parts of the body and the brain itself are interdependent, then there will be a withdrawal from the entire body that "thinks" but cannot be referenced as thought, because this interdependence between the brain and the rest of the body is maintained in a manner at least partly withdrawn from what we normally recognize as thinking. This means that all of the workings of the brain, the spectacular array of synapses and neurons, have a withdrawn dimension that does not reduce to the observation of those workings. Something carries you.

Such a difference — the difference of the double — does seem to follow from the evidence. If nothing else, the reflexes function autonomously from thought, yet they're highly organized in favor of keeping brain and body together. My case has some backing from philosophical quarters, too. From Bryant's perspective, this drive to persist, or *negentropy*, remains withdrawn

---

6   René Descartes, *Discourse on Method and The Meditations*, trans. F.E. Sutcliffe (Harmondsworth, Middlesex, England: Penguin, 1968), 127.

from *every* object,[7] so I'm within an onticological ambit to believe that it remains withdrawn from the human body, even as it eludes direct appearance to a conscious subject in that body.

In Anglo-American circles, one speaks of "other minds" in a similar way. The tiger may not think the *concept* of an antelope, but in stalking one, it is clearly focused on a goal, and the situation involves variables that cause the tiger either to pounce or to wait. The argument here is that the decision suggests the presence of a mind of some kind. Of course, the object-oriented ontologist will go further and make the same claim about, say, water, which we might imagine as forming a droplet on the eaves of a roof. Depending on the circumstances, the droplet may or may not drop to the ground, and this difference traces back to a conserving force that, for all the attributes of wateriness that we might inventory, remains withdrawn. For the most part, I'm in agreement with this view. There's something about H_2O that works to remain H_2O-like, even if from time to time this means turning to steam or ice. What I would like to add to the debate is that the human body has the same kind of conserving agency as other objects do — and another one as well.

Let's put it forward as a thesis: The human object is minimally composed of two virtual beings that withdraw from the same local manifestation. I mean this in a strong sense. In a gentler mood, one could suppose two virtual beings, each of which governs a different part of the body. I'm claiming that two virtual beings manifest themselves in the same part of a human body — that they are colocated. Technically, colocation requires that our virtual beings are not proper, as on Bryant's view, but rather improper — that is, without undisputed title to a place — so I'll be dropping this modifier from here on.

While I may be foolhardy in embracing this thesis, I'm by no means the first to have stumbled upon it. In the Anglo-American tradition, the literature devoted to this peculiar outcome

---

7 Levi Bryant, "Entropy and Me," *Larval Subjects*, March 5, 2012, http://larvalsubjects.wordpress.com/2012/03/05/entropy-and-me/ (accessed June 30, 2014).

is often traced to Locke[8] and falls under the general heading of personal identity. The problem hinges largely on psychological continuity. If I have a memory that stretches back in time, then the persistence of my identity has a psychological basis. Yet I was somehow "me" when I had no memory, and will still be me should I lose all recall. As in the argument I've put forth, there seems to be an animal "me" and another "me." I'm made up of coincident entities, or what some have called too many thinkers.

Note that the reasoning that leads to this excess of thinkers is not inherently dualist. Whatever the variation, dualism asserts a separate and heterogeneous status for mind and body. Here, we're talking about a single body housing two agents distinct from each other. It would be possible, for example, to make a materialistic case for coincident entities. A scientist could look for two superimposed but distinct patterns of neuron behavior, or weigh in on the interpretations of quantum mechanics in which the role of consciousness figures prominently. The dualist could likewise make a psychological argument for the colocation of distinct virtual forces, as Freudians at least begin to do when they pluralize the self into ego, superego, and id. Moreover, in holding the ooo view, I complicate the matter in my own way by addressing agency as an instance of withdrawal, which makes me what's called a non-reductionist (the mind cannot be reduced to the body), but also makes me a non-reductionist for objects in general and therefore raises questions about the kinds of objects that are capable of thought.

All this having been said, most participants in the coincidence debate consider dualism to be off the table because it threatens to reintroduce the existence of souls, or because it precludes any connection between mind and body, and bend their talents instead toward resolving the "ontological danglers"

---

8   Locke's definition, from a chapter that ranges widely over the problem: "in this alone consists personal identity, i.e. the sameness of a rational being: and as far as this consciousness can be extended backwards to any past action or thought, so far reaches the identity of that person; it is the same self now it was then; and it is by the same self with this present one that now reflects on it, that that action was done." John Locke, *An Essay Concerning Human Understanding* (1690), ed. Jim Manis (Hazelton, PA: The Electronic Classics Series, Pennsylvania State University-Hazelton), 318 (accessed January 3, 2015).

that coincidence creates. A leading voice in the pro-coincidence camp is Sydney Shoemaker, a neo-Lockean whose argument requires coincident entities not to share all of their physical properties.[9] Others hold that the logic of too many thinkers is simply incorrect, and that the problem is ill-posed. Eric T. Olson promulgates this view vigorously under the banner of animalism. I hold a somewhat lonely third position, which not only argues for coincident entities that share physical properties, but actively affirms the too many thinkers problem as a fact of the human condition.

Before things get ugly, let me be clear as to what I'm claiming. I'm not developing a theory of the unconscious, at least not in the sense of a passive repository of my formerly conscious thoughts. Nor, strictly speaking, am I advancing a theory of the subject. On my view, my other thinker is an entity that disrupts the traditional binary opposition of subject–object — a parajcct, if you will, or epiject, or any other neologism that conveys the idea of a being *alongside* myself. My other thinker is not me, yet it has a perspective of its own. To use Thomas Nagel's memorable phrasing, there is "something that it is like" to be my other thinker, and this "something that it is like" is not what it is like to be me. And yet here we[10] are, joined at the metaphysical hip. My defense of this position, which for the sake of simplicity I will describe as *colocationism,* most certainly does leave ontological danglers and, in my opinion, very well ought to. Since I've gone on record as a non-reductionist, I should add that I intend to argue this view without recourse to arguments, Cartesian or otherwise, for the existence of a necessary being or prime mover. But, for reasons that will become clear, I also intend to make my case without opposing such arguments, either.

---

9 "To avoid the too many minds problem one must, at least if one is a physicalist, deny that coincident entities must share all of the same physical properties." Sydney Shoemaker,"Persons, Animals and Identity," *Synthese* 162.3 (2008): 313–24.

10 The first person plural is destined to wreak havoc on any discussion of coincident entities. Having broken the rule at the outset, I will try my best going forward to reserve the words "we," "us," "our," and "ours" for instances that include I, the writer, and you, the reader.

A great many essays about coincidence begin with a little mad science. The writer asks: If your brain were transplanted to another body, would your personal identity go with the brain, or would it stay with the body in which it began? The scenario provides a common terminology for both camps, pro and con, without handing a knockdown case to either. The assumption throughout, however, is that the existence of the brain is sufficient for a thinker to exist. My position makes a sort of end run around this assumption, because I hold that the other thinker, the animal "you," is not the brain alone, but rather a force withdrawn from a body that happens to have a brain as one of its parts.

The distinction is not trivial. On my view, once the scrubs are removed and the release forms signed, the animal "you" would resume its role in keeping your parts functioning in concert, but for all that, it would remain inaccessible to you, because it's performing the same function that was inaccessible to you in your original body. That's just what a human body with a brain in it does. If your previous intentions and memories went with the brain, you might have an interesting session in front of the mirror when you were able to get up and about, but there would still be too many thinkers. If, on the other hand, your intentions and memories failed to make the transition, the outcome would be unfortunate, but it would simply resemble familiar scenarios in which personal identity ceases to be, and so leave the argument unaffected, because in every case the entities that are coincident are presumed to last only as long as they do.

The colocationist take on the brain-transplant scenario — where coincidence occurs, it obtains across local manifestations — is at least not ridiculous. But I have other objections to contend with that don't rely on gruesome experiments.

One of these is made on testimonial grounds: If there's more than one of me, why do I always step forward to speak for both of them? By what right do I ever say "I was born" if my personal identity is founded on memories? Why do I say that I am sitting in the chair if two of us are sharing the seat? And who will find the technique to bury "me" in the family plot, if I'm just my memories, beliefs, and desires? While there are sincere replies to this challenge,[11] I personally don't think they need voicing, because people routinely say things that violate clear thinking. When your friend casually says, "it's cold out today," she probably doesn't have the slightest idea what "it" is — because nobody does. Nor should it rank as the defeat of Copernicus if your neighbor remarks at dusk that "the sun is going down."

As objections go, the test of "how people talk" is weak enough that we might actually be content to drop it altogether — except that one of these statements is not like the others. If I believe in coincident entities and yet find myself saying, "I'm sitting in the chair," I might be able to dismiss it as just another of language's many quirks. But after considering the matter further, I would probably not admit to an absurdity, as I would at the oddity of "it" being cold out. In fact, I would probably still say the same thing, because it really *doesn't* seem as if anyone else is sitting in the chair. This leads to a second objection, which Olson calls the epistemic problem.

If your body contained two thinkers, Olson reasons, you wouldn't know which one was which.[12] Since this confusion never occurs, the two thinkers are indiscernible and therefore amount to the same thinker. In the neo-Kantian camp, Christine Korsgaard has mounted a similar defense, arguing that the single outcome of any action is equivalent to the unity of agency. In other words, just as we have a clear impression that only one person is sitting in the chair, it truly appears that only one agent is causing something to happen.[13] Therefore, if we admit that the

---

11 See David Lewis, "Many But Almost One," in *Ontology, Causality, and Mind: Essays on the Philosophy of D.M. Armstrong,* ed. Keith Cambell, John Bacon and Lloyd Reinhardt (Cambridge: Cambridge University Press, 1993), 23–38.

12 "[It] is hard to see how you could ever know which thinker you are, the animal or the person (the one with the psychological conditions)." Eric T. Olson, "An Argument for Animalism," in *Personal Identity,* ed. R. Martin and J. Barresi (Oxford: Blackwell, 2003), http://www.shef.ac.uk/polopoly_fs/1.101685!/file/animalism.pdf (accessed November 11, 2014).

13 I'll engage this line of reasoning with some vigor in chapter four. See Christine Korsgaard, "Personal Identity and the Unity of Agency: A Kantian Response to Parfit," *Philosophy and Public Affairs* 18.2 (1989): 101–32.

epistemic confusion is missing, we ought to concede the existence of only one thinker.

At this point, those manning the trenches of speculative realism will recognize a familiar bugle call: The epistemic argument against coincidence is actually a variant of correlationism. If we were to spell it out in schoolbook form, the argument would run something like this: Logic tells me that another thinking entity exists in my body. I do not experience the thoughts of this other entity (there is no epistemic confusion). Therefore, the logic must be flawed and there is no such entity. As an object-oriented ontologist, however, I feel honor-bound to turn this argument around. Logic tells me that another thinking entity exists in my body. I do not experience the thoughts of this other entity. Therefore, this other entity must have thoughts independent of mine. Since we've invoked Kant, we might, alternatively, take the animal "me" as an instance of the thing in itself, which as friends of OOO know, is the very battle cry for speculation to commence.

In seeking to make the case for colocation, then, my job will be to show that the existence of this other entity — my other thinker — makes a difference to the object that I am, without contradicting the basic outlines of experience. In short, I will have to explain how the thoughts of my other thinker coincide with my *being* without coinciding with my thoughts. This, on the presumption that, if I can learn the slightest bit about my other thinker through our shared manifestation, I might gain a foothold for learning about other objects outside my thoughts as well.

Ironically, another objection gets me part of the way there. On the evergreen subject of pain, Roderick Chisholm presses his case with a horror story of his own. Suppose I'm asked to undergo an excruciating operation under the influence of a drug that induces temporary amnesia, such that I will have no memory of the pain after the fact. Since this operation is cheaper than the alternative, my friends urge me to do it. I'm only myself by convention, they say, so I can easily suppose the person undergoing the operation is someone else. But can I? Wouldn't it still be me writhing on the table?¹⁴ Chisholm constructs his scenario as an argument for the continuity of the person, but in so doing he tacitly suggests the existence of a single entity faced with the prospect of an agonizing experience. After all the conditions are tallied up, only one being feels the pain.

My reply here is to draw a distinction between sensation and thought. To feel pain, after all, is not identical to thinking, because it's possible for me — the "me" who has a memory to lose — to feel pain while thinking something *else*. Is it even possible *only* to experience pain? In moments of physical discomfort, I often have thoughts that don't reference the sensation directly. By the same token, another entity in my body might be able register the pain without thinking the extraneous thoughts that I do. There might, in other words, be a coincidence of thinkers who experience the same pain but *respond* differently. If so, Chisholm's example simply brings my other thinker into view by putting my familiar identity on temporary leave.

This "response differential" can be seen without resorting to special cases. Many people will attest to a sudden crisis during which apparently useless thoughts surfaced. At the moment of alarm, you noticed some peculiar detail — a bird on a nearby branch, or a dent in the snow shovel leaning next to the door — oblivious to the fact that you were already beating a hasty retreat until you heard the sound of your heart in your ears. The onset of shock is actually fairly good evidence of separate human agents. At the very moment when the body is mobilized most clearly to a single purpose, thoughts without any evident relation to that purpose persist.

In addition to the surplus of thought beyond pain, there is ample evidence of the attempt to withstand it. Whether or not you will have any memory of an upcoming operation after the fact, the deliberate effort to conquer the agony of it certainly suggests the existence of two *wills* at work in one body. We don't

---

14 Roderick Chisholm, *Person and Object: A Metaphysical Study* (London: G. Allen & Unwin, 1976), 110–11. Chisholm himself apparently attributed this thought experiment to Charles Sanders Peirce.

see this kind of conflict in many other kinds of objects, and when we do, the inclination is to accord that object some power of thought separate from instinct.

Needless to say, according to some fairly well-known theories, symbolic thought derived from pain forms the very bedrock of psychological continuity. To be unable to have such thoughts is also certainly not to be this sort of thinker. Still, this only secures one side of the issue. If there is a negentropic force distinct from my thoughts that strives to hold my brain and body together, can I really know that it thinks, as opposed to doing something else that is not really thinking?

Does the tiger think? Does my body, when it conserves itself, think? The difficulty is that, by my own definition, the thinker withdraws, making it hard to deduce anything about the internal experience of agents from the identification of distinct behaviors, even if we can establish a quantity greater than one. It's possible to maintain, for example, that what I take to be another mind in my body is simply the body itself. Indeed, science can present empirical evidence of two distinct domains of *memory* in the body, and so seems able to demonstrate multiple agents without resorting to metaphysics at all. This presents a worry from another quarter altogether. After all, if neuroscience supports a physical explanation of coincidence, why bother with the trappings of virtual beings and local manifestations? Why not dispense with whole notion of unseen minds, no matter how many there are in a body, and go straight for the "ism" in materialism, with Ockham's razor in hand?

On my view, two reasons tilt the case in favor of a non-reductive colocation rather than a reductive one.

First, when scientists take the possibility of colocation seriously, they tend to track the passage from conscious thought to unconscious habit, and to ignore the traffic in the other direction. The so-called unconscious memory takes on the menial tasks I'm too busy to trifle myself with, freeing me up to think the More Important Thoughts. Not only does this attitude set up an expectation of servitude from objects in general, it shuts out whatever this other entity might be able to teach the "me"

I know as me. And a receptive attitude toward other entities, aside from being the ground zero of the OOO view, seems intuitively like a good idea.

Second, when science does consider physical causes for consciousness, it doesn't really know what to do with the first-person perspective, with the "me" I know as me. If a study implicates some part of the brain — say, the amygdala — in emotional response, the methodology of the test might be impeccable, and the proof compelling, and still do nothing to explain my experience of an emotional response. A functionalist could go a little further and establish a correspondence between my amygdala and a mental state, but this only serves to highlight the existence of a mental state that's not my amygdala itself. Again, Nagel puts the point well:

> If physicalism is to be defended, the phenomenological features must themselves be given a physical account. But when we examine their subjective character it seems that such a result is impossible. The reason is that every subjective phenomenon is essentially connected with a single point of view, and it seems inevitable that an objective, physical theory will abandon that point of view.[15]

Of course, the biases of empirical scientists don't automatically make my own case airtight. On the contrary, my commitment to the existence of virtual beings entails that one of them never shares my perspective, and there's still something *ad hoc* about this proposal. It may be that there is another object in my body with its own perspective, but just saying so doesn't advance our knowledge very much. Someone could argue that my reflexes are emergent from my parts (say, an aggregation of genes) and constitute an assemblage of adaptive advantages rather than a mind. I could then argue the opposite — we can't say for sure that this same behavior does not constitute a mind — and we

---

15 Thomas Nagel, "What Is It Like To Be a Bat?" *The Philosophical Review* 83.4 (October 1974): 437.

would come to a draw. (Nor should we be surprised at such an outcome, given that we're talking about two different objects — one just a brain, the other a body with a brain.)

Then again, maybe the problem is that we don't still have a good grasp on what we mean by thinking. Another assumption shared by most parties to the debate is that thinking comes in only one variety. If the animal "you" has the same body as you, then it has the same equipment for thinking, so it should have all of the same capacities as you do. So goes the reasoning. But why? An estuary is a body of water in which both tides and currents are present. Both tide and current have the same equipment at their disposal, but we don't for a minute assume they have the same characteristics. Nor, for that matter, do they interfere with each other spatially. So why should it follow that my other thinker is just a straight-up replica of my mental states, if it causes so much trouble to believe it and I can imagine an alternative?

What, for example, if my other thinker were unable to give a report? A certain muteness does seem to be an attribute in every scenario in which the problem is posed. The survival of the body past the personal identity actually defines this difference as the loss of reportability, as does the operation in which amnesia is induced. One could argue that the epistemic objection stems from the same silence: No one appears to be announcing itself, so no one is there. But what if someone actually is there?

If there were thought without language, what would that mean? We can feel justified in saying that the agency that conserves my body, whatever it may be, is *involved* with thought, since its effects coincide with actions that I can call my own, or, perhaps more to the point, actions for which I can be held accountable. On the other hand, if this agent can give no report, then any thinking it does will clearly be of a different order than the kind of thinking that I, the articulating I, can produce. Is there a framework that captures both the sameness and otherness of thought that this apparent colocation suggests?

I would like to propose that a mathematical description of our virtual beings, improper as they are, can provide such a framework where natural languages cannot. The intuition here is that questions about the existence of the mental states closely resemble questions about the existence of mathematical objects. When I think of an equilateral triangle, how big is it? If the physical universe were to end, would numbers still exist? Such questions are not easily answered, and no wonder, since they recapitulate the epic standoff between idealists and realists. Circles and prime numbers really do seem to exist, yet, like our minds, they're almost comically difficult to find. In pursuing the intuition of mental activity *as* mathematical, then, my first aim will be, not to resolve the existence debate so much as suspend it, in hopes of establishing a commonality inside which the various beings of our nature can be described.

2

A Real Class Act

Mathematicians make for unlikely soothsayers. Unlike philosophers, who are still occasionally heckled into submission, geometers speak to us from an airy clime, delivering pronouncements that would put an end to foolishness if only they could be understood. Perhaps this aloofness comes with the turf. Perhaps calculus and Riemann spaces are just too icy for general consumption. Whatever the reason, the decidedly non-populist status of math is strange, because we all use it constantly, and a fairly obscure branch of it at that, as we pass through our days.

The assertion is easily misunderstood. I'm not suggesting that *everything* we experience is mathematical. My phenomenal experience of blueness is precisely what is *not* mathematical about the color blue, since blueness doesn't occur to me in terms of quantified frequencies, spectra, and the like. On the other hand, as already noted regarding pain, I never experience *only* blueness. I always experience blueness along with other phenomenal experiences, and it's the relation between such experiences that, I propose, is essentially mathematical.

What I mean by this is that thinking can be characterized minimally as the activity of sorting. We group this with that. We separate one thing from some part of another. Blueness goes here, yesterday's rainbow goes there. Behind the pageantry of hopes and fears, we're tenaciously arranging our impressions of the world. On my view, this penchant for sorting makes each of us not only a mathematician but a specific variant called a *set theorist*. Not that we can rattle off the subtle rules of set theory on demand, of course. Like Monsieur Jourdain, who was surprised to learn from his tutor that he'd been speaking in prose all his life,[1] we happily employ set theory all the time without knowing it.

Inaugurated in the late 19th century by Georg Cantor, set theory begins with the almost diabolically simple relation of belonging. When objects are collected, the group they form is a called a set, and the objects so collected are said to belong to it. Over the course of set theory's development, it became necessary to organize this central intuition into a number of axioms in order to avoid certain basic logical contradictions, and from these axioms great cathedrals of mathematical thought have been raised. There's more than one way to resolve the basic contradictions, however, so there's more than one *model* of set theory, with some variation in the axioms asserted. The most widely accepted model is known as Zermelo-Fraenkel set theory, or ZFC, so named for the mathematicians who elaborated it, and one reason it's so widely accepted is that it works with every other branch of mathematics, from arithmetic all the way up to the most abstruse developments in the field. Whether you're going through a grocery list or deriving a complex algorithm from the traffic patterns on the New Jersey Turnpike, ZFC set theory will be doing some of the work for you.

Interestingly enough, ZFC isn't just the glue holding times tables and topology together, either. In addition to its broad underpinnings, it has made its own contributions to the repository of mathematical knowledge. At the very outset, for example, Cantor gave rise to no little astonishment when he proved that there are more real numbers (say, the points on a line) than there are natural numbers (1, 2, 3, …), even though both of these sets are infinite. The existence of transfinite sets — sets larger than "simple" infinity — has radically changed the course of mathematics and led to sobering conclusions about tradeoffs between completeness and consistency in any system of thought. It has also led to a ban of the very idea of totality. Once you have larger

---

[1] Molière, *The Middle Class Gentleman* [*Le Bourgeois Gentilhomme*], trans. Philip Dwight Jones, http://www.gutenberg.org/files/2992/2992-h/2992-h.htm (accessed February 4, 2015).

infinities, you can have larger infinities than that, and so on without surcease. If nothing else, this creates problems for Descartes' ontological argument that what conserves you is all-knowing.[2]

The field is still not entirely settled, however. While some of ZFC's axioms are uncontroversial, others continue to stir uneasily at the edges of mathematical pursuit. And it turns out that the troublesome axioms are the very same that ones that will merit our closest attention as we try to resolve the problem of colocation.

Up until now, I've been pitting my argument against analytic philosophers, largely because they've been the most vigorous contestants in the debate over coincident entities. In turning to set theory, it's mostly the Europeans — Alain Badiou, and more recently Quentin Meillassoux — who have applied set theory to the question of being outside thought, and it's partly from them that I'll be taking my cue. But there are also a great many actual set theorists producing interesting results, who have not an ounce of curiosity in French philosophy, even though they speak the same formal language. In particular, I'm alert to the findings of Joel David Hamkins, who argues for a mathematical multiverse[3] in which no single model of set theory prevails. If you believe in a multiverse, you don't seek truths that necessarily hold in every possible world, so much as investigate the processes that connect and separate worlds. You don't just take ZFC at face value. You tinker with it and see what happens if you remove this or that axiom.

---

2 For an excellent overview of set theory, see Joan Bagaria, "Set Theory," *The Stanford Encyclopedia of Philosophy* (Winter 2014), ed. Edward N. Zalta, http://plato.stanford.edu/archives/win2014/entries/set-theory/ (accessed August 15, 2016).

3 Note that a multiverse is not the same thing for a set theorist as it is for a physicist. See Joel David Hamkins, "The Set-Theoretic Multiverse: A Model-Theoretic Philosophy of Set Theory," The City University of New York, The College of Staten Island of CUNY & The CUNY Graduate Center New York City, Philosophy and Model Theory Conference, Paris, June 2–5, 2010, http://lumiere.ens.fr/~dbonnay/files/talks/hamkins.pdf (accessed December 16, 2014).

The multiverse view is very much in keeping, not only with the OOO stance on the equality of objects, but also with the conundrum of coincident entities, because each model of set theory is defined as a specific set of axioms, and some of these axioms have been revealed to be *independent* of the others. Independence in this context means that a given axiom can't be generated from the other axioms of the model, or, to put it another way, that the model is consistent within itself, whether the axiom in question is included in the model or not.

The suggestion, which I now intend to develop into a sound argument, is this: Insofar as thought can be expressed as the mathematical operation or exercise of a specific set of axioms, we can suppose our virtual improper beings to be distinct mathematical *operators* with different models of set theory at their disposal, which is to say operators with some axioms in common and other axioms exercised exclusive of each other. Going on this hypothesis, I will construct different models for our two thinkers, both of which are intelligible even when the correlationist view is well defended. Obviously, these models will not be the only models one can construct. But if I build them well and present a reasonable case that they reflect our intuition of what our two thinkers could be, it will set the stage for a further possibility — that we can overcome the correlationist view, not by actively seeking the other thinker's thoughts, but by rendering them *independent* from our assumptions about them. To the extent that these other thoughts have consequences by virtue of their independence, this procedure will then put us in a position to exist on an equal footing with another entity, who walks when we walk and squints at the sun when we do — who lives, quite literally, in our midst.

Who Goes There?

Since my argument for colocationism proceeds from evidence about bodily responses, my first task will be to tease out some feature of motor activity that gives us a hint of axiomatic difference. To raise the stakes a little (or lower them, you decide), let's set aside scenarios that might involve clinical shock in favor of a more mundane example — some case at least several steps removed from any personal experience of pain. Say I notice that my cat has jumped onto my desk, close to a cup that sits beside an important stack of papers. Knowing that the cup is full of coffee, but not thinking very clearly about my cat's cognitive skills, I shout, "watch out," move across the room and pick up the cup. The cat jumps away, and life continues...

The broad outlines of the issue have already been posed: For all the apparent simplicity of this scene, some undetermined surplus of the *action* remains withdrawn from me. I can say I picked up the cup. I might be able to articulate several smaller units of my act — that I turned, moved toward the cup, and put my left hand on the handle, if that indeed was the case. If someone filmed me, the footage might give greater detail again. No one, however, myself included, can describe every *decision* involved in the action. I'm compelled to offer clunky accounts. "I turned my shoulders as I looked at the cat, and shifted my weight to my right foot." This exposition might be accurate, but it leaves out a lot, even for the brief segment of the act it's supposed to cover. So even if there only seems to be one of me engaged in an action, there's an explanatory limit to my willing of it, beyond or beneath which the execution actually takes place. What lies beyond this limit? To answer this speculative question, I'll be bringing set theory into play as promised. But first, a brief foray into the empirical research on locomotion will help set the stage.

Nikolai Bernstein was a self-taught scientist of the Soviet era who, despite his isolation (or maybe because of it), had a major impact on the field of motor learning.[4] Among Bernstein's contributions was to articulate what is known as the degrees of freedom problem. Humans and animals, he observed, have available among their body parts more combinations of choices

---

4 N.A. Bernstein, *The Coordination and Regulation of Movements* (Oxford: Pergamon Press, 1967).

than are needed for any task—in fact, an infinite number of combinations from which to choose.

In raising the prospect of the infinite, the degrees of freedom problem calls up familiar paradoxes about runners and the impossibility of completing a supertask (which dividing by halves to reach a goal surely is), but the situation here is even more complicated than that. Not only does the runner have the course to traverse, she also has decisions to make about which arm to lift first, how high to raise the knees and so on, each of which contains innumerable variations of its own. More than a supertask, motor activity is super-multitask. What Bernstein did when faced with the prospect of a super-multitask was to turn Zeno's famous argument around and produce a different question. Given that we do reach goals, he asked, why do we have such an overabundance of means for doing so, and how does the body navigate this forest of options?

Bernstein's work led to an explosion in motor studies, especially after the demise of Stalin, who distrusted the ideological implications of his findings. For our purposes, several points emerge. First, the study of the problem itself is undertaken from a perspective outside the actual experience. It doesn't seek to retrieve any *awareness* of the many infinitesimal motions, or any report of why some motions are made at the expense of others. It may be said that this perspective still gets us no closer to identifying micro-motor activity as thought. Maybe it's not strictly necessary to choose one motion over another. Maybe the body simply feeds back perception about the target until it's reached. However, this objection only says that *I* didn't make the choices, not that the choices were never made. The argument here is similar to the case for other minds, in which the tiger chooses to attack or not. In fact, it's a refined version of the same argument, since there are variations where I might choose not to pick up the cup after all—for example, if that cat jumps off the desk before I get there. But in any event, Bernstein's exterior perspective is helpful, if only as a reminder that I do not have access to the organizing force behind the activity, even though it's in my own body.

Moreover, we can see that these motions *are* organized, even when marshaled to tasks without any clear instinctive motivation. Bernstein and many others since[5] have shown that motor activity exhibits efficiency by targeting the *parts* of an action. These parts, called synergies, are no more consciously executed for being more manageable. They fall rather into the category of habit. You shift your weight forward before stepping, or learn to place your thumb over your curled fingers "just so" in order to hold a hammer. Over time, you become more adept at running or driving nails.

So much might seem trivial to assert, but to say that synergies emerge from an infinite array of choices actually helps us to clarify our notion of coincident entities because it lends itself to a set-theoretic perspective. The implication, in short, is that whatever holds brain and body together amounts to a mathematical operator (and therefore to a thinker) because it assumes the validity of a set-theoretic axiom called the axiom of choice. Moreover, this mathematical operator makes this assumption *on its own grounds*. I emphasize the point because the axiom of choice stands at the threshold of "our" side of conscious accountability.

Roughly speaking, the axiom of choice addresses the problem of selecting something before you know what it is. Although mathematicians initially overlooked this problem, it became necessary to reckon with it when dealing with the vast entities that Cantor brought into view. For a finite set, a rule for choosing is easy to establish, because the set has already been inspected in advance and deemed countable. The natural numbers aren't too scary, either, because I know I can reiterate the same successor operation to the limits only of my own fatigue. But what about that seemingly solid thicket of real numbers between 0 and 1? I can't even make a rule for counting these elements, because each two elements will have another element

---

5   For just one among many of the recent discussions in the field, see Lena Ting and J. Lucas McKay, "Neuromechanics of Muscle Synergies for Posture and Movement," *Current Opinion in Neurobiology* 17.6 (2007): 622–28.

between them, such that I can never apply a choice function to all of the elements. If I suppose I can select the smallest element first, I will be defeated as soon as I realize that there is no smallest number between 0 and 1. So I need a fiat: "If I want to choose any number between 0 and 1, it will be there."

This fiat is the axiom of choice. In one of its simpler forms, it says: "The product of non-empty sets is non-empty." Another formulation emphasizes selection: "Assuming a set of bins each of which contains at least one element, it is possible to select exactly one element from any bin." But however it's formulated, the axiom of choice also allows us to say: "An infinite set contains a countable subset." This assertion is especially interesting, because it looks a great deal like the claim that synergies of motor activity — parts of an action — emerge from an infinite number of options.

While we're mulling over this parallel, it should also excite our curiosity that the axiom of choice has been proven to be independent of the other axioms of ZFC (which is why the C, for "choice," is dropped sometimes, leaving us with plain old ZF). Its independent status means that the axiom of choice cannot be accepted on the basis of set theory itself, but must be accepted according to some *other* grounds. We have to leave the crystalline aerie of mathematical models to find justification for stealing parts from infinity. As sufficient reason to do so, mathematicians generally cite convenience, because a great deal of their work simply can't be done any other way.

The instinctive mind, on the other hand, seems to take the axiom of choice for granted. As the cat jumps onto the desk, my body is already moving through a branching of options that defy analysis in their infinitude. Whether I prevent the cup from being knocked over or fail to do so is beside the point. The intuition is of an operator that does not experience doubt. The virtual being that organizes these myriad choices seems to behave as if a next choice will always be available, no matter which pathway is taken or how many subdivisions of movement it finds. It doesn't act as if there are any gaps in existence. It acts in innocence as if the world exists — that something will be there ahead of any existing information.

Here is where I believe set theory can again help to increase our knowledge. Because we know that an operator is deriving countable subsets from infinity here, we know that the axiom of choice is involved. As it happens, we also know that another equivalent statement for the axiom of choice is: "the set of real numbers *with the empty set removed* has a choice function."[6] The empty set is simply a set with nothing in it, a group without content that offers nothing to sort. If you think about the real numbers as being entirely "full" and never lacking content — that is, not being empty anywhere — then it seems clear enough that any choice function placed on them will yield some kind of content.

On the strength of the foregoing, we can venture a hypothesis: Where an operator A has a given choice function on motor activity, and where motor activity takes place within the domain of real numbers, operator A does not require the empty set. To make the formulation stronger, we could say: If A *always* has a given choice function on motor activity, and motor activity *always* takes place within the domain of real numbers, then A does not *encounter* the empty set. This hypothesis is supported in turn by the generally accepted observation that muscle activity is never entirely at rest, but retains some electrical potential, even at its least energetic. The motor mind knows only motion, and, what amounts to the same thing, knows only positive being.

In isolating our elusive mathematical operator this way, we've hit upon a few simple identifying features that give us some explanatory power as to how it behaves. As it encounters the environment, it meets each stimulus with a response, leaving no remainder. A set theorist would say that the set of stimuli and responses is well-ordered. This is because a least element,

---

[6] The assertion about real numbers follows from the established equivalence to the axiom of choice: "For any set A, the power set of A with the empty set removed has a choice function." A power set consists of all of the subsets of a given set. Since the power set of the natural numbers is made up of the real numbers, the inference is straightforward.

by which we mean an *earliest* response, is always available, even if extension in space is continuous.

One could quibble with the quantifier "always." It may be, for example, that operator A recognizes the empty set every now and then, and therefore needs to borrow the axiom of choice from grounds other than its own (in order to apply a choice function to the real numbers). One might argue against the continuum of space, on the grounds that extension is not necessarily made up of real numbers. I believe the case is strong enough, however, to make a first commitment to a set-theoretic model for our other thinker, namely, that the axiom of choice is always among its operations, while the axiom of the empty set (i.e., that there *is* an empty set) never comes up for review.

At this point, complaints might also arise from quarters having nothing to do with set theory. What about constraints on the body itself? One can hear the analytic crowd mustering their paraphernalia. What if you were strapped to a gurney with iron manacles on every extremity, rendering you unable to move? What if your limbs were all cut off — what would become of your parsimony of response in a case like that? Admittedly, motor activity is limited in certain circumstances. However, even in highly constrained cases, some withdrawn entity will continue to *behave* as if the options were infinitely large. We would do well in this regard to recall the phantom limb phenomenon, in which the amputee has the impression of being able to move the lost limb. My conscious mind will have the impression of something other than itself being engaged in a super-multitask — even when the vehicle for carrying it out isn't there!

Another challenge to the innocence of our other thinker is the specificity of its medium. Doesn't the human anatomy favor some stimuli over others in such a way as to render a flat ontology unattainable? Most object-oriented ontologists place a good deal of importance on the differing constraints of an object. The bee sees thousands of flowers where you or I see one. The dog hears a much higher tune than you or I. To privilege our own particular constraints, the object-oriented complaint might go, is to privilege the human over other objects.

I agree with the insight behind this complaint, but it's not clear that it affects my position. It's certainly plausible that different objects will perceive the world differently, even if they enjoy the one-to-one relation between stimulus and response I'm describing. In such a case, we suppose that they receive different stimuli from each other and respond according to their bodily constraints (their degrees of freedom). The mathematical operator at work would only go as far into the continuum as needed in order to respond. This, in fact, is the very charge I laid against ooo in the beginning, when I held that the acceptance of caricature across beings does nothing to refute correlationism. But remember: The being I've been describing, though it shares my body, is still not *me,* and the challenge at hand is not to defeat correlationism in *others.* It may be that the minds you and I actually inhabit, as opposed to this one that we have just identified, stand as rare cases among the panoply of virtual beings where such a defeat is even imaginable.

The small scope of my description might also seem problematic. A well-ordered set of stimulus and response doesn't necessarily encompass the entire human object, insofar as the human object undergoes processes that are beyond kinesthetic activity entirely. It doesn't necessarily have any bearing on the production of insulin or the growth of hair, even if it indirectly affects those processes. In this sense, its existence can't give a complete answer to Descartes' question "What conserves me?" It may, however, show coincidence between entities within the limits of motor response, and in the strictest sense, motor response is precisely the domain in which *practice* can be undertaken.

We've made some headway, then, in defining the other virtual being that persists in withdrawing from my personal identity. This virtual being does not propose the existence of objects and then set out to find them. Like my cat, it cannot re-orient my words "watch out" to wonder if I've left a timepiece in the yard. In short, it does not — and we will suppose it cannot — attempt to look outside the sets that are presented. It responds to what is presented, whether the stimulus is internal (say, hunger) or external (whatever hunger identifies as food). Yet it also has a dizzying number of responses at its disposal. Where this combination of the assumption of being and the subdivision of uncountably large sets appears, it will lend strength to the supposition that the axiom of choice, and therefore a thinker, is involved. Drawing from an existing tradition of cognitive science, which categorizes motor responses below the level of consciousness as organized by implicit memory, I propose to call this thinker the *implicit mind,* and the model at its disposal the *implicit model.*[7]

Implicit knowledge is often described as "knowing-how," as opposed to explicit or declarative knowledge, which attests to "knowing-that" — and conveniently enough, the latter term is just as apt. (Generally, neuroscientists who use these terms are straightforward materialists and far removed from debates about coincident entities. My contention, obviously, is that these two kinds of knowledge indicate two different minds.) Like the cat in my example, my implicit mind exhibits significant degrees of freedom and yet is able to assume the axiom of choice in a way that I find problematic in my own cogitations, but by the same token it lacks certain capacities that my personal identity assumes with ease, the most obvious of them being the ability to give an account — to make declarations about my experience.

Who's Asking?

How, then, might this other ability, this *declarative mind,* be explained? The question is no less daunting for finding ourselves once again at home, as it were, with explanations. In trying to characterize the implicit mind, we came up against a certain otherness that resisted personification. For the declarative mind, the opposite holds true: We run the risk of over-personifying it. It may be a fool's errand to give an account of that which can

---

[7] The term "procedural" is often used to describe one kind of implicit memory, and it's preferable in some ways to the term "implicit." But Ian Bogost has already adopted the term "procedural rhetoric" to mean something slightly different, so I will avoid it where possible in order to prevent confusion.

give an account, unless the idea is to affirm that all such efforts are foolish. On the face of it, that's perfectly true. On the other hand, we're often called upon to give an account of our actions with some appeal to their basis. If someone were to ask me for my account of picking up the cup, she probably wouldn't be asking me how I did it, but why, or at least not completely how, and at least partly why. So we are faced with a problem that's not limited to philosophers. Moreover, we've gained an inkling of the scope of declarative thought by identifying the axiom of choice as independent of the other axioms in ZFC. Is there, then, some connection between this uncanny otherness of choice and the basic tools of reportability?

Taking an account to be language-based, broadly construed, I propose that we'll find a path from letters to numbers (and back again) through the principle that the mathematician Akihiro Kanamori has called *indifference to identification*.[8] This principle will be familiar, on one level at least, to semioticians. As Saussure pointed out at the dawn of structuralism, one can use any sound or symbol to refer to an object. The small number of onomatopoetic words in use worldwide only demonstrates the point: Signifiers *can* resemble what they signify, but the resemblance is by no means necessary. The mind that can formulate words is able to substitute one sound or image with another *indifferently* to the ontic particularities of the object in question.[9]

That signifiers are arbitrary is obviously an important insight about the ability to give an account, but it's also significant that indifference to identification can be used to apply the same function to different objects, or to seemingly different objects. The cup on my desk and the cup that my cat accidentally broke yesterday are different in one way but the same in another. Each actual cup, which is distinct from every other cup in the world, is called a *token,* while a cup "as such," as a category, is referred

---

8 Akihiro Kanamori, "In Praise of Replacement," *The Bulletin of Symbolic Logic* 18.1 (2012): 47.

9 Ferdinand de Saussure, *Course in General Linguistics,* ed. Charles Bally et al., trans. Roy Harris (Chicago and La Salle: Open Court, 1986).

to as a *type*, and can be used to consider many different cups indifferently.

As the mediator between types and tokens, indifference is therefore able to address a wide range of philosophical concerns. Not only does it capture a basic function of metaphor ("love is a rose"), it's almost indispensable for logical rules of inference. When we say, "All men are mortal, Socrates is a man, therefore Socrates is mortal," we silently employ indifference to advance that the token "Socrates" is also of the type "man." Moreover, even "one" object can be considered a type rather than a token, since it exists in different instantiations over time. A cup that survives from morning to afternoon may be considered different in some way and still rate as the same object, at least as far as my report of it goes.

The rift between continental and analytic philosophy can be traced in large part to commitments as to which of these two applications of indifference should win the day, with one side wielding ever more transgressive adjectives and the other posting warning signs around the properties. I have no inclination to take sides in the dispute. On the contrary, when both applications are used at once, there's a certain lockstep effect that will show itself as my case draws to a close. What I want to establish for the moment is merely that the principle enjoys these two uses in relation to language — indifference to the signifier on one hand, and indifference to the signified on the other — because this will allow us to make the move from names to numbers.

In set theory, the axiom that addresses indifferent to identification in both of its uses — whether I want to assert the equivalence of the words *Tasse* and "cup," or I want to claim the equivalence of a new cup to the one my cat broke yesterday — is the axiom schema of replacement.[10] In the vernacular, the axiom

---

10 "Replacement can be seen as a crucial bulwark of indifference to identification, in set theory and in modern mathematics generally. To describe a prominent example, several definitions of the real numbers as generated from the rational numbers have been put forward [...] yet in mathematical practice there is indifference to actual identification with any particular objectification as one proceeds to work with the real numbers. In set theory,

schema of replacement says: "If an element in a set is replaced with exactly one another element, the result will be a set." Normally, the substitution is described as a formula or function that's "mapped" onto a set. If A is the set of natural numbers, I can map a function f onto A to create a new set, B, in which each natural number bears the function f. Say, for example, that I work out the equation for the graphic shape of a cup. I apply this function to my set, and *voilà*: I get one cup, two cups, three cups, and so on. I get the cup as a type. The natural numbers have become signifiers.

Strictly speaking, the number of functions that might be enlisted for a replacement set is limitless. If I get tired of mapping my "cup" function onto A, I can switch to any other function that captures my fancy. This will be helpful for my account, which is probably going to be made up entirely of signifiers, and in fact, it seems self-evident that an entity capable of language can employ the axiom of replacement at its leisure. Those who have availed themselves of Ian Bogost's Latour litanizer will also appreciate the point.[11] Using replacement, I can generate the signifier *apples,* or — just as easily — *car parts, burnt toast, dentistry, the state of Idaho,...* the list can easily be made to match any litany of objects given by an object-oriented ontologist as warranting equal status with each other.

Unfortunately, the use of replacement comes at a cost. The axiom tells you that the substitution of an element in a set will give you another set, which professional set theorists need if they want to establish sets like the unions of infinities (say, the

---

one opts for a particular representation for an ordered pair, for natural numbers, and so forth. What Replacement does is to allow for articulations that these representations are not necessary choices and to mediate generally among possible choices. Replacement is a corrective for the other axioms, which posit specific sets and subsets, by allowing for a fluid extensionalism. The deepest subtlety here is also on the surface, that through functional correlation one can shift between tokens (instances, representatives) and types (extensions, classes), and thereby shift the ground itself for what the types are." Kanamori, "In Praise of Replacement," 47.

11 And those who have not, are encouraged to proceed without delay to http://www.bogost.com/blog/latour_litanizer.shtml.

union of the set of odd numbers and the set of even numbers), and which ordinary mathematicians like you and I need if we want to give labels to objects. But even though the axiom is unfettered in terms of the functions available for use, any function chosen is still *a* function, and because there's no *a priori* choice for any next substitution, problems show up at higher levels, where one function is presumably meant to have a relation to another through some overarching function that connects them. Once I've generated the natural numbers, I can always use replacement in the Saussurean sense, by using another formula to derive the graphic shape of a cup, without worrying about the particular shape I chose. So far, so good. I can represent cups in my style, and you in yours. Everything changes, however, once it's granted, as we already have, that a report will always leave something out. Between my perception of my cat and my decision to stand, both of which I can explain as types, there's a gap that my account is unable to fill.

The supposition here, for the sake of satisfying our assumption about the correlationist impulse, is that substitution is in progress whenever thinking occurs — that thought for the mind I inhabit *is never without* the operation of substituting one set for another, even if it returns the answer "same set." This gives us the neatness of the Cartesian ego, which exists whenever it's thinking, but it also implies something very odd. What can it mean, after all, that thoughts are discrete enough to be recognizable, if they are *continuously* replaced with other thoughts? Something must change the input at points along the way, such that one arrives at sameness or difference over time. (Note that I'm not asserting the need for the *world* to be stable. I'm simply making an observation about how the declarative mind behaves.) If language is "always already there," as the continentals say, and the act of substitution is co-extensive with declarative thinking, then each successive moment will present the opportunity to *sort* — either to assert some new mapping function, or to hold good with the one currently under consideration. We can see that something does this selecting. Something "digitizes the analog," otherwise we would not recognize our own thoughts — but what?

It might be put forward that this something is the implicit mind itself. Maybe I don't need to make an explicit choice for where one object begins and another ends, because — one might argue — the implicit mind takes care of it for me. There's a rather large cultural industry dedicated to the premise that human consciousness can be naturalized along these lines, and we certainly see as much in cases of procedural learning, at least on one level. The fingers come to know the violin better than I do, as the implicit mind isolates synergies from an infinite array. But the idea that my implicit mind can *become* whatever agency lies in the gap loses strength as soon as we add innovative combinations of predicates into the mix. If, for example, still following my leitmotif involving cat and cup and papers, I get the bright idea of putting my cup somewhere else besides my desk next time, the implicit mind will not be the driving agency, because "next time" is, strictly speaking, never presented, and the implicit mind as I've defined it can't register what's not there.[12] Yet I can remember that I planned to move my papers to a different location, and I can recognize it as a good idea at a later date, even if I haven't gotten around to doing it. From here, it's easy to see that the same will hold for any thoughts that involve rules of inference.[13] If the implicit mind were the only bridge between one state of awareness and the next, I would be a very different kind of creature than the one I am.

Well, then, suppose I introduce my personal identity as a single "master" predicate that justifies *any* function I might choose next. So much would allow me to consider "everything

---

12 Such a case actually works better than one involving the direct experience of pain. In the direct case, we might suppose that the implicit mind retreats from a painful stimulus as a matter of habit, and so assigns a new home for my papers just by happening onto it. But here no pain actually arises from the papers themselves, so the adaptation cannot be considered in the same way.

13 As might be expected, replacement does the heavy lifting here. Where (a), (b) and (c) are subsets, and (c) = "on my desk," replace (c) with (d) = "on a high shelf."

that is predicated" with impunity, since it could be organized by the very act of me thinking it. And why not? There's certainly a sense in which the continuity of my identity across functions is inescapable. Even writers who argue against psychological continuity try for a consistent argument, and they sign their name with some uniformity from one article to the next. On the other hand, the continuity of my identity seems impossible to attain, since I need to start with a type — myself at different occurrences — in order to make a rule for all types, including the rule for *myself* over time. If I attribute my identity to an additional factor (say, some intermediary that provides the ability to share instances of memory between instances of my identity), I get no further, because I still require this additional factor to persist and so to produce some overarching type — for as long as it does.

This vicious circle has posed a problem for psychological continuity ever since Locke first claimed that personal identity is defined by its sameness over time, among the earliest objectors being Joseph Butler, whose argument came to be called the circularity objection.[14] Indeed, the vast majority of arguments about personal identity look to solve the grounding problem that this circularity provokes, rather than bothering themselves, as I am, with the situation of too many thinkers at the same time. The circularity objection remains important for the colocationist argument, however, because it gives us an entry point for clarifying the challenges faced by *one* of my coincident thinkers.

And challenges there are. If, as the correlationist argument dictates, predication is constitutive of the declarative mind, I have problems beyond my choices of where and when to limit objects. This is because whatever it is that projects sameness or difference into the gaps in my report must do so on the strength of some mapping function, even though one of the things that

---

14   Joseph Butler, *The Analogy of Religion, Natural and Revealed, to the Constitution and Course of Nature. To Which are Added Two Brief Dissertations: I. Of Personal Identity, and II. Of the Nature of Virtue* (Oxford: At the University Press, 1849), 303–11.

has to be projected into the gap is… an operator actually capable of employing a function. After all, I can clearly recognize instances where my thinking, conscious mind stops and then resumes again, and not only in obvious cases, such as when I sleep, but also when I stand or fiddle with a pencil—or put my papers where I've never put them before. The clunkiness of my account dogs me wherever I go, and reinforces the weird feeling that I'm myself only in fits and starts. So if I'm committed to believing that I'm the same person before and after these discontinuities, even if only in some partial way, then I must believe in some substrate that binds together not just memories or recognition of objects, but instances of my own *perspective*—of what it is like to be me.

There must be an operator that ferries me through the fog to meet myself on the other shore, because I do arrive on the far bank somehow. Yet nothing in my own repertoire can reproduce what it is like to be me, so any such "bridge operator" is simply not available. So long as I want to be capable of the simplest species of reason, then, I have no recourse but to *construct* my own continuity, the complaints of Joseph Butler and company notwithstanding. The result will not be instantly satisfying. To reproduce continuity, it must be the case that I've somehow constructed a version of myself that is itself capable of constructing myself (so as to be the same as me), which version can in turn construct myself constructing myself… and onward into the mist. Of course, this series is impossible to complete, and therefore it can never be constructed—and aside from its dazzling aspect, a series that is both necessarily constructed and never constructed is sure to keep my troubles from ending anytime soon.

This brings us, by a route that I hope has not been too tortuous, to the axiom of foundation. Early set theorists were blissfully unaware of the need for this axiom, because they assumed the ability to assign a predicate to any set. If they wanted to assign the predicate "cup" to all cups, they just did it, and that was that. Then Bertrand Russell came along and wondered about a set that does not have itself as a member. Defining a set in this way raises an insurmountable paradox once you consider the set of *all* sets that do not have themselves as a member, since this set must have as its members sets that are not members of it. If I'm thinking about the cup on my desk, the thinker that I am can be easily excluded from membership in this set. The set contains a cup and a desk, end of story. But if I then escalate to "every thought I have," I'll surely need to include the thinker that I am, since I've admitted to its existence in a largest set just by asserting its exclusion from a smaller set. Run every variation on this argument you like, you end up with a contradiction — the same contradiction that's triggered by an operator contained within its own operations.

The main takeaway from Russell's paradox is that there can be no set of all sets, and that when you claim to have found one, you're actually looking at something called a *class,* which is simply a group of elements that unambiguously share an attribute. For the most part, set theorists don't like to deal in classes, for a reason that many ordinary people will also find compelling — as soon as you ask what's in them, you find yourself down the rabbit hole, where things are not what they are, and are what they aren't.[15] But the correlationist, who believes that thought encompasses all being, cannot be done with classes so easily.

ZFC's solution to self-belonging, and to the problem of classes generally, is the aforementioned axiom of foundation,[16] which, simply put, requires every set to have an element that remains disjoint. An element must exist with a relation to a set without belonging to it. Usually, this so-called *foundational* element is taken to be smaller than the smallest element in the set, the tra-

---

15 Tim Morton rejects concerns about Russell's paradox outright, and in fact vigorously embraces the idea of things being what they aren't. As already stated, my strategy, like that of Meillassoux, is to find a solution from inside the correlationist circle, which on my view is intimately bound up with self-belonging. It's in this spirit that I accept both the paradox and the law of non-contradiction. If I can win the hard case, so much the better.

16 Technically the axiom of separation solved the problem of self-belonging first, and foundation was added as a means of further defining the solution — not so much to explain that sets can be separated as to explain how they can be separated.

ditional example being the empty set, which contains no thing and is always waiting "down below" the non-empty, no matter how far down the chain of being you go. A non-empty set will, of course, not be *in* the empty set (or it would not be empty), while the empty set can be added to any non-empty set without incident. The same could be said for three and any set of whole numbers greater than three: I can find three cups in any set of cups of four or greater, but finding four cups in a set of three will be hard work.

We might wonder, then, if the empty set can break the chains of self-belonging where my personal identity only seems to wind them in ever more binding coils. We've already had an inkling of this possibility in the ability to consider objects that aren't present. My papers aren't currently up on a shelf safe from damage, but I can imagine it as being the case. The empty set, which is what we get from the set containing both my papers and the shelf, seems to be crucial for any kind of thinking beyond rote habit. Indeed, my use of it not only allows me to consider changing my habits (putting my papers on the shelf and leaving my coffee on the desk), but to think, say, "all of the jaguars in this room" — of which there are currently none — and many other things that don't exist besides, including objects that are yet to be. I can think of this book as complete, for example, even though the complete book does not exist as I type these words. I'm able to make plans, even the best laid ones, thanks to the empty set.

Encouragement fades, however, when I try to use the empty set as the foundation of my thoughts. If I suppose that the empty set founds what I think by being unthinkable, then I won't be able to see that "all the jaguars in my room" is a fiction, because I won't be able to recognize the set so described as empty. Any substitution will be just as real as any other. To make this work, I would have to eliminate language or accept complete delusion. If, on the other hand, I suppose that the empty set *is* thinkable, it will belong inside the set of things that I can think and will therefore not be foundational. To round out the possibilities, I might suppose that I never think anything *but* the empty set and that every other thought is composed of it. One imagines here compositions built from nothing, as when set theorists generate the natural numbers from the empty set. In this case, though, I'll be sorely pressed to show that there are different things in the universe by virtue of the empty set alone (even if they're only thoughts of different things), because the empty set is not different from itself. So long as I am able to think difference, my identity must be active even in the face of so-called emptiness.

Another option, and not necessarily the final one, is the prospect of "outsourcing" my bridge operator. Maybe another entity altogether, completely exterior to my colocated organism, can provide a foundation that doesn't trace to *either* of the minds in my body. The idea is a potent one, in that it ranges from the basis for a Theory of Mind (the idea that other people have minds at all) to philosophies of Otherness in general. We might hope here for a proof of being outside thought. If the world was there when I went to bed and still stares back at me when I wake up, doesn't it mean that the world necessarily exists beyond me? It does, of course. The world, or any part of it I may recognize as persisting, can only count as a truly exterior bridge operator, however, if I lose my identity altogether. For me to think of *myself* as continuous, it still must be the case that I somehow insert an image of myself across the gap, which then revives the recursive appearance of yours truly and the ensuing problem of self-belonging.

Unless — a final hope exerts itself — what if I predicate each and every conscious moment of myself as belonging to this exterior bridge operator? I expand its powers beyond the gap and into the clear and distinct activities of my days. The vicissitudes of being an ordinary mathematician drive me to identify with some entity larger than myself. I'm not just me, I might say. I'm the son of my parents, a writer, the citizen of a nation, etc. But then, there it is again: Because I construct at least the part of this larger entity that warranties my own *recognition* of my identity on either side, my choice of it is subject to the same circularity that haunted my personal identity to begin with!

If I wanted to make the correlationist circle tough to breach, set theory has certainly helped me out. The mind I inhabit thinks in types ("this is a cup and so is that"), yet it has to *be defined* as a type in order to maintain the consistency of other types ("I'm the same person as the person who started this sentence"). The operation persists at the brink of nothingness and continues up to the largest encompassing entity I can imagine. More to the point, I'm faced with a tradeoff: Insofar as replacement obtains *reflexively,* foundation fails. Of course, we would expect no less from the correlationist premise: If everything is predicated, nothing can be disjoint from predication. But we now have some additional information. Where nothing is disjoint from predication, I will either have constructed an "I" that cannot be constructed, which looks suspect, or I will have introduced a halting point to the infinite regress of "me's" by constructing a bridge operator that constructs me in turn.[17]

The declarative mind is thus as precarious as it is prodigious. It can plot the landing of a machine on Mars or conjure all the jaguars in a room, but whatever its astonishing feats, it's caught in an anti-foundational maze, which entails not only the expected foreclosure from the "great outdoors" (to use Meillassoux's winning phrase) but also a certain anxious resistance, not to physical death, but to the loss of logical consistency. Although in the last instance an account is supposed to be coherent, it's actually built from a contradiction that's forever ready to unravel into random bits of representation: the entropic event of the personal identity. And it's precisely *this* outcome, as distinct from our physical absence from the universe, which we actually cannot think, because the negentropic drive of the declarative mind is, plain and simple, to preserve the soundness of the account.

---

17 It could also be said that I partly construct a bridge operator that constructs me in turn. The distinction revives the main issue of correlationist debate — whether an object (in this case, an entity I'm calling a bridge operator) exists independently of my thought. While I'm holding to the stricter formulation here, I will be pushing the point of partial construction in chapter four.

The model that arises from this drive, the *explicit model,* has at least some identifying features that distinguish it from the implicit mind. Unlike its coincident counterpart, it relates one set to another through the constitutive activity of replacement, even to the point of predicating nothingness. Yet it can't employ the axiom of choice on its own grounds, because it doesn't *have* its own grounds. It is, in short, just the kind of customer that drives the object-oriented ontologist crazy: a thinker that privileges thought over being, to the point of resisting the possibility of any existence outside its own predications, even at the cost of that ontological dangler I promised: Some entity, somewhere along the line, can't be what it is and can only be what it's not.[18]

That concludes my account of coincident entities as mathematical operators. The distinction I'm making between implicit and declarative minds makes intuitive sense, and, I believe, delivers a reasonable reply to several of the objections to coincidence in a fell swoop. We can see why two thinkers in a single body might think in ways that are inaccessible to each other and still have access to a common source of perceptual information. It's not absurd for me to be unaware of what another thinker in my body is thinking, because the driving axioms at its disposal lead to a fundamentally different kind of thinking. At the same time, I can understand something about what this difference is, because my other thinker is operating in a formal language I can recognize. The implicit and explicit models also allow for both thinkers to "occupy" the same place, because they are mathematical operators, which give us no compelling reason to worry about their collision in space. Nor is the price for the thesis too high to pay, since it merely affirms experiences we can recognize as our own. Colocationism is consistent with the observation that the animal "me" can persist beyond the collapse of my identity, that we can both feel the same pain, that I can have an

---

18 By no means do I claim this maddening non-identity as an original finding. Sartre, for one, said it early and said it well. As with many other points in this essay, my method is to follow the consequences of the argument first, and let the chips fall where they may.

intuition of unhesitating being, that I can feel bound within my thoughts, and that the shadow of failure attends my account at all times.

Admittedly, I've left out several important details. For the sake of simplicity, I haven't gone into detail about the ZFC axioms that both thinkers can be expected to share.[19] Nor have I made any pretense of explaining how colocation comes to be, or came to be, or whether it is a case peculiar to humans. On the other hand, the very provisional nature of my account leaves the door open for further exploration. Someone might, for example, use these models as a springboard for a theory of thinking objects that allows for a spectrum of mathematical capabilities, comparing and contrasting — and perhaps combining — them with other models of ontic difference.[20]

Then, too, many aspects of the colocation thesis will not be problematic unless you think they are. You could spend a lifetime not caring how many thinkers you possess, or what mathematicians might have to say about the universe. Certainly, anyone is entitled to think in classes rather than sets. But it will be hard to trumpet the object-oriented view as accomplished if you agree that human object is complicated in the way I have set it out. It will not be enough, for example, to say, "All objects equally exist, including humans," because the statement smuggles inequality back in merely by being made. To be the maker of the list is to be the founder of the list, in the mathematical sense that it is included in every object on the list. Presumably some of

---

19 For the record, the remaining axioms are: extension, pairing, union, separation, infinity and power set.
20 An obvious point of departure is Jacob Von Uexüll's theory of the *Umwelt*, but empirical science is also continually providing live threads. For example, the finding that plants employ math in rationing their starch production in response to interruptions in a normal diurnal light cycle, and experiments showing that newborn chicks appear to associate higher numbers with their right side, just as humans do. See Heidi Ledford, "Plants Perform Molecular Maths," *Nature News*, June 24, 2013, http://www.nature.com/news/plants-perform-molecular-maths-1.13251 (accessed February 1, 2015); also, Rosa Rugani et al., "Number-Space Mapping in the Newborn Chick Resembles Humans' Mental Number Line," *Science* 347.6221 (2015): 534–36.

these other objects have their own foundation for existing. So if I would like the term *human* to mean a mathematical operator who could possibly make a list, I mischaracterize these other objects according to whatever image of the operator I have.

This mischaracterization will apply to my interpretation of my other thinker as much as it does to anything else. Derek Parfit has argued that the status of our identity in the future qualifies as a special concern, and then proceeds to show how this special concern is based on incorrect reasoning.[21] Apparently, our anxiety about the collapse of the account serves the same purpose: I have an interest in the predicate of my identity prevailing in the future as the same predicate that I assert now. But if what I'm saying is true, we humans have *two* special concerns — one for the declarative mind, another for the implicit mind — and it's not at all obvious that they agree. In my effort to harmonize my actions with my personal identity, I might mischaracterize my body in such a way as to override the special concern of my other thinker. On the other hand, it may also be that the special concern of my declarative mind, which Parfit seeks to allay, might be best allayed if a means were found to enter into some kind of exchange with my other thinker, which, according to the model I have advanced, does not have a *long-ranging* concern for its future identity.

Of course, I'm already guilty of overwriting my other thinker in this very way. I've advanced that the human object has two virtual beings in one manifestation, and I've allotted attributes to each of these beings. Not only that, I've assumed that one mathematical operator bears the character of some vaguely mammalian mind — from the perspective of a mind beset by self-reference. But I still might not be wrong. It may still be that some telltale operation of the implicit mind can be loosed from the mind I inhabit, if only I could find the right way to proceed. Russell himself saw the frailty of this hope when he wrote:

---

21   Derek Parfit, *Reasons and Persons* (Oxford: Clarendon Press, 1984).

> The [paradox of self-belonging] is, however, purely negative in its scope. It suffices to show that many theories are wrong, but it does not show how the errors are to be rectified. We can not say: "When I speak of all propositions, I mean all except those in which 'all propositions' are mentioned"; for in this explanation we have mentioned the propositions in which all propositions are mentioned, which we cannot do significantly. It is impossible to avoid mentioning a thing by mentioning that we won't mention it. One might as well, in talking to a man with a long nose, say: "When I speak of noses, I except [sic] such as are inordinately long," which would not be a very successful effort to avoid a painful topic. Thus it is necessary, if we are not to sin against the above negative principle, to construct our logic without mentioning such things as "all propositions" or "all properties," and without even having to say that we are excluding such things. The exclusion must result naturally and inevitably from our positive doctrines, which must make it plain that "all propositions" and "all properties" are meaningless phrases.[22]

The import of this passage, written shortly after Russell discovered the antinomy that bears his name, has cast a long shadow over philosophy. On the Anglo-American side, one sees the stirrings of Wittgenstein's commission to remain silent about that which one does not know. The continentals have learned for their part to be cautious about assertions of totality, at least within the bounds of human interactions. For the object-oriented ontologist, however, silence about the wilderness of being won't do, because it tacitly awards knowledge a totality that it hasn't earned. To make matters worse—for me anyway!—positive claims about the wilderness of being won't do, either, because they just go ahead and cultivate the wilderness despite their best intentions. So what's a poor object-oriented colocationist to do?

---

22 Bertrand Russell, "Mathematical Logic as Based on the Theory of Types," *American Journal of Mathematics* 30.3 (1908): 226.

Fortunately, the math that got me into this mess can also get me out. Rather than professing to know — or not to know — anything about beings that are not me, I propose to enlist set theory itself as a means of excluding propositions of totality, and so of delivering what could be called a flat practice. For reasons that will become clear in the following chapter, I will refer to this exercise as *grounds forcing*. In the interest of nailing the case for colocation, I'll be training my attention on the implicit mind first. But because, no matter how many minds I have, I patently do not comprise the sum of all being, I'll also be led to apply the same extracted principles to other objects — to develop procedures of *extended* grounds forcing.

My first step along this road will be to think big without plotting world domination. On this point, I'm very much in accord with Tim Morton, who favors the very large over the "ever more infinite infinite."[23] Seeing that my problem, at least at the outset, is that my mapping functions are unrestricted, I will try to identify a class that's smaller than "anything I can think about" and then look for a strictly defined mapping function that's *probably* not part of this class. If it's not part of this class, it will show itself by its lack of any limiting relation: Within the class, it will fail to map anything but itself. It won't stand for anything, or indicate any consequence inside the class under consideration. It will be a choice function without defining relations except to itself over time — a *monotype*. Yet this monotype will not for all that turn out to be the empty set, because that would once again allow for the class of everything. The idea is then to see how large a set can be formed from this class before it falls apart.

Such a project admittedly meets up with a challenge: how to choose this inconsequential predicate. If I choose it, haven't I already betrayed the cause, right at its birth? I've begun to make things right by limiting myself to some area of thought that

---

23 "[I]t might be harder to imagine four and a half billion years than abstract eternity. Actuality presents us with disturbingly large finitudes. Quantity humiliates. The other appears in this world, not beyond it." Timothy Morton, *The Ecological Thought* (Cambridge, MA and London: Harvard University Press, 2010), 40.

explicitly contains less than everything.[24] So long as my limit holds, I can theoretically choose a monotype that, on the one hand, lies outside "less than everything" and on the other, cannot be chosen within it. So much would prevent circular reasoning for any attempt to relate the monotype within a proscribed domain of thoughts. Still, how to know where the borders of inside and outside lie?

I will try to meet this difficulty by homing in on a class, all of the members of which share some predicate x as well as some unsubstantiated predicate of *necessity,* which together will show up as that bridge operator that I pair myself with so as to rate as a continuous entity. From there, I'll look for a monotype that appears to be completely contingent according to predicate x — and add it to this class. Within such a class, the monotypical object will, obviously, have no basis for being, and it will also have no limiting relation among the other objects in the class. So my monotype will not only be monotonous, it will be the very picture of contingency. And to the degree that I can limit my contribution to the capabilities or imaginary powers of the monotype, I will also know that to think it within the class is to not think myself as its mathematical operator. Conversely, where operations do result from this exercise, I will know that another operator is bringing them about independent of my thought.

The real test of this auspicious pronouncement will involve some additional technical machinery, which, as mentioned, is coming up soon enough. For the moment it suffices to highlight the modifier "over time." Because by definition the monotype is not necessary — it only exists or does not — it shouldn't matter where it appears among the thoughts of necessity. I won't have to decide where it belongs. The only way to verify such complete mobility, though, will be to introduce it into the class on an ongoing basis, breaking each part down in order to expose any hidden "need" to eliminate it. As a result, necessity will be expressed,

---

24 Left here, this strategy would basically be what set theorists call limitation of size.

not as eternal, as a logician would normally use the term, but as *imminent*. (Not to be confused with *immanence*; I mean imminence in the conventional sense of "about to happen.")

We begin to see now how stalking the wild implicit mind diverges from other recent projects involving set theory. Badiou, the incumbent continental thinker on the matter, uses set theory to intercept an event that not only is named but unabashedly belongs to itself, and to which the subject is related by fidelity.[25] For my part, I see set theory as a means of blocking the paradox of self-belonging so as to decenter the human, leaving faithfulness to plurality. What's more, if what I propose can be made actual, there would be no need to search for an event, because it would be available at any time during the course of everyday life, wherever the particular range of necessity is asserted.

I've also mentioned Meillassoux in connection with set theory, and one might be tempted to draw parallels between my monotype and his *kenotype,* or meaningless sign.[26] Because signs are unmotivated, Meillassoux argues, he is able to employ combinations of them without forgoing their meaninglessness. These kenotypical expressions, because empty, can then be expected to describe reality without the intercession of thought.

While Meillassoux has obviously been instrumental in the emergence of the speculative trend of which OOO is a part, I intend to keep my own counsel here. I agree that his proposal captures the Saussurean sense of indifference to identification, in that any sign could just as well be written $\{\backslash |\}$ or $\{:::\}$. What he seems not to realize, however, is that his empty *sign* serves the same role as does the empty *set,* which says "nothing here," whether it's written as $\{\emptyset\}$ or $\{:::\}$ I've already cautioned against the hazards of asking the empty set to describe reality. By the same token, to combine different kenotypes in order to derive specific results about mind-independent reality (a process he calls reiteration) is in my opinion to suppose differences that are not meaningless, but merely hidden.

---

25 Alain Badiou, *Being and Event,* trans. Oliver Feltham (New York: Continuum, 2005), 506–7.
26 Meillassoux, *Iteration, Reiteration, Repetition.*

My proposal accordingly offers something less grandiose: to consider known but limited domains of imminent necessity, into which one can introduce in each case a non-empty signal (internal or external) that resists relation, and continues to resist that relation upon dull iteration — that is, without variations on its form. This approach, as I have already suggested, is consistent with the multiverse view of set theory, because it doesn't claim a master meaningless sign for thinking everything outside myself, but rather settles for different domains for decentering my perspective, each of which can be evaluated for its independence from other domains, and for how far it maximizes its reach.

It might be urged that, in advocating dull iteration, I'm lobbying for good old-fashioned ignorance. Am I tacitly opening the gates for the revival of a transcendent being, to whom we should surrender our cherished control? The question is a good one, considering the immediacy with which the correlation of the master predicate reasserts itself. Theoretically, of course, I run no risk of playing the dogmatic proselyte if I can continue to maintain the independence of my meditation from *imminent* necessity. Freedom from the next imperative is, strictly speaking, the very defeat of transcendence on the ground. I will, however, be constrained from issuing the sort of edicts one commonly sees when an argument is being defended. Indeed, I will meet contradiction whenever I *insist* that this or that truth must be admitted, or acted upon, or conveyed to others with the fleet speed of stallions. If I'm to rest my case on a type that implies no other types, there is simply no basis on which urgency can be invoked. A monotype will not be "for" anything, and so cannot come to be on the basis of its need to be. It will exist, when it does exist, without sufficient reason.

On this point, I do draw from Meillassoux, who uses the existence of transfinite sets to argue that contingency supersedes the necessity of stability in the universe.[27] My variation on this argument, with which I concur, is simply to apply it to thought rather than to the world out there. Set theory disables

27 Quentin Meillassoux, *After Finitude: An Essay on the Necessity of Contingency*, trans. Ray Brassier (London and New York: Continuum, 2009).

the existence of the set of all sets and gives us as consolation a foundational element disjunct from every set. Therefore, given a class predicated as necessary, which is normally enlarged by predicating a more encompassing necessity, I contend that it's still *possible* for this class to be exceeded by an element that isn't necessary, which is to advance the possibility of an element that organizes this class of thoughts into a larger set according to the principle of contingency.

In this respect, my proposal lays out a welcome mat for atheist and believer alike. Think of it like this: If you believe in an omniscient deity, you'll probably believe that you yourself do not have complete knowledge. (And those who believe they *are* omniscient will know where I'm going with this.) My proposal remains neutral as to the deity you believe in and instead intercedes on your belief in the incompleteness of your own knowledge. If you really do believe your knowledge is incomplete, then you will have no complaint. But if it turns out that you do believe your knowledge is complete, then my approach will demonstrate that you are wrong, and that you've been laboring under the delusion of your own omniscience. Such a demonstration should not affect the actual existence of an all-knowing entity one way or the other, since it only exerts itself on claims of totality, which, given a conservative size of the universe, are likely to be based on a very small part of it, leaving plenty of room for contingent entities larger than you before the knowledge of everything is reached. If there is a god, my method won't break any of his furniture.

Granted, my argument as developed so far hangs on the slender thread of asserted possibility. To be persuaded that this possibility is more than wishful thinking, the patient reader will want to see a case where necessity not only presents itself, but where it definitively fails and, just as crucially, where its quarry is taken up again outside our mastery. Since I've argued for the colocation of virtual beings in the human body, and more specifically as they express themselves in motor activity, it's to motor activity that I now turn to substantiate the rumors I've started.

3

Stalking the Wild Implicit Mind

If you search the web under "Alexander Technique," you're apt to find a variety of sites depicting persons in the glow of good health and color schemes that run decidedly toward the pastels. Among the testimonials lending gravitas you might find one by the pragmatist John Dewey, who was one of its early and abiding advocates. All in all, though, you're likely to get the impression that the technique has something to do with stress reduction. This is true enough in its way, but the main point is somehow lost, as if Darwin were remembered as a travel writer with a good eye for detail.

In the interest of full disclosure, I should say that I took lessons in the Alexander Technique for several years.[1] I have no bona fides beyond that, however. I'm not an Alexander teacher, I'm not especially good at it, and in fact, I don't even plan to address the technique as it's taught on a daily basis. Instead, I'll be limiting myself strictly to the thought experiment that inspired it, as detailed by F.M. Alexander himself in his book, *The Use of the Self*.[2] In isolating my scope in this somewhat fundamentalist way, I hope to steer clear of debates over which variation (if any) deserves to be sanctified as authentic, and to capture instead the broader implications of his initial discovery. No doubt I'm courting controversy even so. If nothing else, the colocation thesis flies in the face of some of the theoretical claims that

1 My teachers were Ted Dimon and Jane Tomkiewicz.
2 F. Matthias Alexander. *The Use of the Self: Its Conscious Direction in Relation to Diagnosis, Functioning, and the Control of Reaction,* 3rd ed. (Bexley: Integral Press, 1946). See especially chapter one, "Evolution of a Technique," 1–25.

Alexander subsequently made to support his teaching, which tend toward pronouncements of control and mind–body unity. Yet there's encouragement in seeing that my approach leaves the heart of his discovery untouched, and the benefit, too, that it sets the stage for applying it to other areas in life where decentering the human might be of interest.

In the waning years of the 19th century, Alexander was an actor with a modestly promising career ahead of him, except for one problem. Whenever he went onstage, he found himself losing his voice and making gasping sounds. He consulted an expert and, not surprisingly, was given a variety of exercises to perform. These exercises yielded some success — until he went onstage again, at which time the gasping and rasping returned. The process continued. He exercised offstage and relapsed when the curtain went up. Finally, when a doctor suggested another round of exercises, Alexander asked an obvious question: If the problem goes away when I'm offstage and reappears when I'm onstage, doesn't it stand to reason that the problem lies with something that I'm doing when I'm onstage? The doctor had no satisfactory answer, and so Alexander, good man of progress that he was, decided to undertake a grand project.

Central to this project was a mirror. Specifically, Alexander studied his reflection in one for years. When a single mirror proved insufficient, he got two more. It bears noting that from the very beginning, he regarded himself — body and mind alike — strictly as an object. He didn't regard the mirror as a metaphor. He didn't ask himself if he had a hidden motivation for losing his voice. He didn't try to visualize his body in some new way. Instead, he asked himself, "How does this thing, the human body, work? What is happening with the vocal cords, the feet, the shoulders — right now?" Although it would be covetous to call him an object-oriented ontologist, he was certainly oriented toward objects, foremost among them the human one.

Alexander began his "mirror phase" by observing any physical differences between his speaking and stage voices. One of the first things he noticed was that, when reciting, he tended to throw his head back, depress his larynx and suck in air. He noticed, too, that he did these same things to a lesser degree during normal speaking. After more observation, he isolated the act of throwing back his head as the action that caused the other two problems, and set about trying to stop himself from doing it. But his own impressions failed him. In fact, by looking at his reflection he was able to verify that, whenever he thought he was moving his head up and forward,[3] he was actually continuing to pull it back and down. Worse, even after he had learned to move his head up and forward, he was literally unable to do so in the moment he tried to speak. Back and down went the head.

We would do well to underline a point here that, while often made in the Alexandrian community, is not, in my opinion, generally given the emphasis it deserves. Although Alexander was unaware of it at the time, his physical reaction was identical to the startle response, or startle pattern, which occurs most markedly on a sudden stimulus such as a thunderclap or gunshot. The startle pattern is observed the world over, across every culture, and is thought to be a reflex for protecting the back of the neck. Here is a succinct description of it:

> *[T]he reflex starts with the head* which jerks as the neck muscles contract and the eye muscles tighten and blink. Then the response moves down into the torso which flinches; the shoulders raise and arms stiffen, the abdominal muscles contract and the chest flattens, then the knees flex — all this in around one second. Alongside these external changes, breathing and blood pressure levels change and the heart rate accelerates. Interestingly, the response begins with extension and immediately changes to flexion.[4]

---

3   The spatial orientation of "up and forward" is easy to misunderstand. "Up" in the Alexandrian parlance refers not turning the face toward the ceiling, but rather to extending the spine, such that the top of the head moves further away from the body. "Forward," for its part, means to tilt the head forward as the spine extends along the back of the head — as opposed to, say, extending the head out in advance of the body.

4   Hilary King, "Definition: Startle Response," http://www.hilaryking.net/glossary/startle response.html (accessed June 30, 2014), emphasis my own.

Alexander went on to observe the startle response at work, to a greater or lesser degree, in any motion he might make. As he began teaching others, he confirmed this same response many times over, as did his students, who included the likes of Aldous Huxley and George Bernard Shaw. Eventually, one student, Frank Pierce Jones, undertook a series of formal experiments in which he established the startle response as paradigmatic of poor kinesthetic use throughout the general population.[5]

But the pervasiveness of the startle is not the unexpected finding. What's surprising is that *one's own* speech is able to trigger it. Whatever it is that seeks to keep brain and the rest of the body together responds to an ordinary activity within its purview as a *threat*. As with Bernstein's observations on the degrees of freedom, the insight is made from a perspective outside the body. By looking in a mirror or, say, watching a video, I'm able to see that two different stimuli — internally produced speech and an externally produced sound (say, a thunderclap) — elicit the same physical response. So unless I'm willing to deny that the standard physical response to a threat reflects the recognition of *another* being, I'll be compelled to admit that Alexander's problem demonstrates the existence of coincident entities.[6]

This mismatch between command and response also puts a crimp in the case for sensation as the ground of human activity. Earlier, I argued that the implicit mind can't provide continuity for my perspective across the gaps in the declarative account,

---

[5] Frank Pierce Jones, *Body Awareness in Action: A Study of the Alexander Technique* (New York: Schocken Books), 132–33; 148. More recently, experiments entirely outside the Alexandrian community have borne out Jones's conclusions. The neuroscientific literature on the startle response is quite extensive and deserving of further attention from philosophers, but for the main point here, see J.S. Blouin et al., "Interaction Between Acoustic Startle and Habituated Neck Postural Responses in Seated Subjects," *The Journal of Applied Physiology* 102-4 (April 2007): 1574–86.

[6] One might raise the objection that autoimmune responses also provide evidence of a body set against itself. But no one has said that the body can't go wrong, and even if it's true what Williams Burroughs says and language is a virus from outer space, then its colonization is fairly well accomplished at this point.

simply because it can't offer some of the capacities that need to be continuous. The argument at that point was a logical one. Here the argument gains strength from empirical quarters. I look to sensation to tell me where my head is in relation to my torso — and sensation is wrong. I think I'm doing one thing but I'm actually something else. The word Alexander liked to use in describing the state of the typical adult sensorium was "debauched." In a less Calvinist mood, we might say that the senses are drawn into the correlationist circle. Thought overrides being at their nearest encounter.

Certainly Alexander discovered that mere exhortation to be aware of his body was not enough to make it so. Once he realized how poorly matched his ideas and their execution were, he came up with a new plan: He would refuse to carry out the specific command (or stimulus) to speak and then renew his command to let his head move up and forward. This refusal to act he called *inhibition* (some years before Freud cornered the market on the term) while the iterative renewal of "head up and forward" he gave the name *direction*. Having established these two specific kinds of thoughts, he broke down the means of carrying out the command to speak into parts, always renewing his direction with each part. The steps were quite precise: He inhibited part 1, then part 1 and part 2 together, then parts 1, 2 and 3 together, and so on, silently reiterating the direction of "head-up-forward" at every step, until he had thought through the means for achieving even such a humble goal as saying a few simple words. He referred to this cumulative process as "all together, one after the other."

But even this cumulative process, detailed as it was, was not enough to keep what Alexander referred to as his "habitual self" from pulling his head back and down. He found that he also had to inhibit the hidden necessity of *any* goal, and so devised the so-called flank movement. At the point where he had thought through the means of carrying out a command, he stopped and considered whether he wanted forgo his goal and continue as before, to continue on with his goal, or to do something else entirely — renewing "head-up-forward" for each case, as always.

In other words, he gave over his thought as best he could to suspending many pre-determined goals at once while maintaining the directions at every step. At this point, finally, he was able to speak without pulling his head back and so overcame a difficulty that "had beset him from birth."

If nothing else, Alexander's thought experiment shows how complicated the task of dull iteration can get. Just to give himself one simple command, he had to re-examine everything he did. Small wonder, then, that he steered his students away from the full-blown version, with its flank movement as a closer, and instead developed a teaching method in which he used his hands to guide them through most any ordinary motor activity *except* for speech.[7] And indeed, the Alexander Technique proper, as he came to teach it, demonstrates something quite amazing all on its own — that one implicit mind can communicate to another through the material of bodies. Yet Alexander also insisted that the difference that resulted could only be achieved through conscious reasoning. Even if the student didn't go through every step of the process outlined above, the teacher did, and the effect then "knocked on," like one billiard ball to the next. Moreover, his exposition of his discovery is a remarkably detailed account of someone treating an activity entirely as a series of thoughts to be sorted, and so lends itself well to recasting in set-theoretic terms.

The term I've given to the demonstration of an independent operator coincident with me is grounds forcing, and, since I now intend to put it to work, it's high time I explain what I mean.

Stated in natural language, forcing is a notion of set theory in which an element is introduced into a set in order to generate a new set with unexpected properties. Normally, these properties involve the behavior of the axioms of set theory itself, and

---

[7] Alexander's sorties into formalized lessons involving utterances extended only as far as a procedure called the whispered "ah," in which phonation and even basic syllables are expressly avoided.

indeed, the first use of forcing, by Paul Cohen in 1963, demonstrated the independence of the axiom of choice from the other axioms of ZFC (showing that set theory was consistent with or without the axiom of choice). The technical intricacies of forcing are famously maddening, as those who have tried to learn it know well.[8] Fortunately, I get to begin from a demonstrated fact and then seek to explain it, rather than identify a specific notion of forcing (of which there are now many) and then strive to fit it over the demonstrated case. Granted my approach is unorthodox. Set theorists might be inclined to interpret the following passages as what happens when Caliban gets hold of a calculator. But so long as we hold to the basic idea of generating a new set in a semi-controlled way without knowing its makeup in advance, we can proceed with confidence, and with an open invitation to our mathematician friends to judge whether the exposition that follows qualifies as forcing, or rather deserves the title of some other mathematical procedure.

Broadly speaking, Alexander located a command that did not belong to a certain class — the class of his commands resulting in actions — and subjected this class to a series of formal operations until the execution of the command passed from the impossible to the contingent. In terms of set theory, he reduced a class to a certain kind of partly formed set and then added an element to it — which is what we mean by replacement — so as to force the appearance of a new set that he himself did not choose — and never could have chosen.

The first step in this journey is simple enough. Alexander identifies a goal: to speak. Let's call this goal A. In order to reach it, he considers the words he intends to say, the recitation techniques he has learned and the various motor activities he might need along the way. Since he's also evidently thinking of *himself* as intending to speak, we would, given everything we have seen

---

8   Paul Cohen, "The Discovery of Forcing," *Rocky Mountain J. Math* 32.4 (2002): 1071–100, http://projecteuclid.org/euclid.rmjm/1181070010 (accessed December 15, 2014).

about language and self-belonging, say he's dealing with a class that unambiguously shares the attribute of his personal identity.

Having identified this goal A (to speak), Alexander then attempts to let his head move up and forward — a command that we will designate # — while trying to execute A, and finds it to be impossible. Note that # is a non-empty set. It has content. We wouldn't say, for example, that he's seeking to empty his thoughts, as in Buddhist meditation. Nor is he seeking any state as general as mindfulness. He's trying to cause a specific positive outcome.[9] With this in mind, he reasons that something must be wrong with the way he's going about his task, this class, A, that prevents the desired outcome from occurring.

His next move also has a mathematical cast: He tells himself *not* to carry out A and to proceed with #. This decision gives him a little more clarity. We can easily see that the refusal of a command has the value of 0 and the assent to that command has the value of 1. By inhibiting an action — by strictly refusing to respond to a stimulus — he has thus turned the class A into a closed interval $\{A_1, A_0\}$, where A_1 is the command to speak and A_0 is the suppression of this command. Both of these terms cannot obtain at the same time, so he knows that they're not the same — and he knows there's an interval between them containing something. He just doesn't know what that something is.

This new plan works… sort of. The union of A_0 and # succeeds, and # occurs: If Alexander does not try to speak, he can direct his head up and forward. Nevertheless, the move from A_0 back to A_1 returns the previous result of $A_1 \cup \# = \emptyset$. So long as he refuses to speak, he can perform the action that will allow him to speak!

Of course, between 0 (the inhibition of the action) and 1 (the active command) lie the real numbers, which, as we know, defy enumeration. Like Nikolai Bernstein, Alexander is unfazed by

---

9   No doubt the union of A and # delivers what set theory calls the empty set, but as with the case of "all the jaguars in this room," emptiness here simply means that A and # have nothing in common. Either Alexander speaks, or he lets his head move up and forward, but there is no instance that includes both — and Alexander definitely wants an instance that includes both.

the dazzle, and just dives right into this infinity, looking more closely at his inhibited action and breaking it down into the parts he actually experiences. In set-theoretic terms, he begins to identify subsets of A. Whenever he locates a motion that contributes to the goal A_1, he refuses to obey the command to execute it, just as he has done for A_1 itself. In this way, he generates a series of closed intervals, which we can show as $A = \{a_1, a_0\}$, $\{b_1, b_0\}, \{c_1, c_0\}\ldots$.

We might pause again for a moment, this time to appreciate that Alexander is undertaking an empirical experiment on the first-person perspective, *dismantling* what it's like to be Alexander, from within that very perspective. His refusal to respond to each of the subdivisions of A throws the workload squarely onto his internal mental processes. Rather than the actions, he's looking for the *commands* that lie between silence and speech. Yet he isn't looking for a master command behind these commands any more than he is aiming for emptiness. He's not trying to locate himself. Instead, he just takes each stimulus as it comes and pairs it with its negation, in search of a physiological result.

Interestingly, if Alexander can maintain a strict either/or status for each for these paired subsets, he will be adhering to the law of the excluded middle, which is equivalent to the axiom of choice. And, just as interesting: His ability to execute either command — to respond as well not to respond — stands as the definition of contingency: "It's possible that a_1 comes to be and it's possible that a_1 does not come to be."[10]

None of his attention to contingency would amount to much, though, were it not for the drumbeat of replacement he applies to each pair in turn. Unlike the various commands he considers, he never conceives of # as one of the actions to be negated. He only thinks # → #, which, with its unimaginative mapping

10 In logical notation: $\Diamond a_1 \wedge \Diamond {\sim} a_1$. It's the sign of a marvelous planet that one can actually find a paper on it discussing the correspondence between modal logic and forcing, and showing that if ZFC is consistent, forcing extensions can only attain the level of the necessarily possible. Joel David Hamkins and Bendikt Lowe, "The Modal Logic of Forcing," *Transactions of the American Mathematical Society* 360.4 (April 2008): 1793–817.

function, is what I've been calling a monotype. He simply projects, no more or less, that he will move his head up and forward when he tries to speak. Since every other command is divisible (as demonstrated by yielding some subset between 0 and 1) and since by stipulation # is not divisible in this way, the clear result is that # does not have any subsets. It has no internal relations that can be witnessed. Alexander is thus able to test whether any subset surreptitiously includes ~# by continuing to think the opaque # at every step. As soon as he draws his head back, he knows that some hidden command has prompted the action, and he can subdivide further until he locates the hidden command, which can then be negated in turn.

From a naive standpoint, this makes sense. He sees that he can move his head up and forward as long as he doesn't try to speak, so he wonders whether some *part* of the action might be causing ~# and begins testing all of the parts in order to isolate the culprit. The empirical dimension of his efforts becomes finer grained.

Even now, though, there doesn't seem to be a culprit. Or rather, the culprit lies not in any one part, but across the entire class A. Is it possible that there are spaces *between* subsets where ~# silently resides? He tries to rule this possibility out by locking down each new subset and then including it in the previous one. Formally, he is now creating a *partially ordered set,* which places the relation ≤ on the temporal sequence of his subsets. For any earliest subset that he locates and negates, he continues to think #. He considers this subset along with #, then the *next* available subset combined with the first, refuses to execute both of them, and again thinks #, in the cumulative process he describes as "all together, one after the other."

In natural language, this process is quite cumbersome. Crazy as it might seem, Alexander thinks, "Do not open the mouth, but let the head move up and forward… now do not open the mouth but let the head move up and forward *and* do not curl the tongue but let the head move up and forward…" As a formal matter, the relation of ≤ is a something more beautiful: a description of the unfolding parts of an action without committing to a decision about the continuity between them.

Unfortunately, crazy or beautiful, even this isn't good enough. The partial ordering process continues until Alexander arrives at A_1, at which point he selects A_1, including all of the inventoried subsets leading up to it... and the result comes back ~# yet again.

So what's going wrong? Of course, he might be missing some hidden subset, since the possibilities appear to exist along a continuum. He has no way to find it if this is the case, because at a certain point he will exhaust his power to discern subsets. On the other hand, he can consider whether A itself is simply *too small*. This, too, makes sense, since the command to speak doesn't exist in isolation, but always appears along with other commands: to stand, to remain standing, to sit, to look out the window, and so on. The class A is never the only class presented. All tasks are in some respect super-multitasks, and there remains the chance that some other task will be linked to the command to pull his head back and down.

Even if Alexander is motivated simply to find some way of letting his head go up and forward while he speaks, he is therefore led by his frustrations to consider larger possible sets of actions. How far can he go, he wonders, in his exploration of tasks? What if he proposes another action in addition to speaking? What if he includes the possibility of doing neither of these, and simply continues on as before?

Insofar as he has become interested in *any* motion he might make, Alexander is now considering not only $\#\{A_0, A_1\}$ but also $\#\{B_0, B_1\}$, $\#\{C_0, C_1\}$,... $\#\{X_0, X_1\}$ — meaning, closed intervals up to and including any hypothetical motor command at his disposal. This addition of the element # to *any* action amounts to the full-blown use of the axiom schema of replacement, which is required anew each time an element is to be added to a set among an infinite number of sets. One result of this decision is that Alexander relinquishes his idea of the completion of A_1 as the only event of importance. Where before he concerned himself with the commands *within* the completion of A_1, he now considers commands that lie outside it as well: He's no longer committing solely to speaking. Moreover, the flank movement involves not only a larger inventory of commands, but also what he does *before* he attempts to speak, including, crucially, whatever he is *already* doing.

The abrupt revelation is that stillness does not exist. There is always at least some element between no motion and the next motion. At the same time, he has accumulated a series of motions he cannot perform.

What unfolds next shows how the grounds for his action are forced. If the desired effect had occurred by thinking an action from *within* a closed interval, Alexander would have demonstrated his own use of the axiom of choice, since he would have chosen from a continuum. But this is not what happens. Instead, he opens up a competition between several different commands, each enjoying its own closed interval. Of course, as is ever the case with replacement, his addition of the monotype # must be axiomatized for each of these commands, and as we have seen, such a procedure would normally set off a spiral of self-belonging, with the need for a bridge operator to hold all of the commands together. In this case, however, because he's necessarily already engaged in one of the proposed actions — to which, by his own admission, he does not have access — "he" cannot move. Some other, unnamed choice function is thus *forced* to select a path forward, creating a new and larger set, each step of which includes #. The result is that the head lifts and brings with it those subsets that will come, leaving alone those that will not, and Alexander speaks.

We can see more clearly how this unnamed choice function exceeds personal identity once we recognize the flank movement as an example of diagonalization. This is the method that Cantor used to prove that some infinities are larger than others — for example, that the real numbers make up a larger set than the rational numbers. In our case, diagonalization serves a method rather than a proof, but the structure remains largely the same. In the standard proof, one starts by assuming that the set of real numbers is *not* larger than the set of rational numbers and then tries to find a contradiction that defeats this assumption. So, for our part, we generate a wish list of numbers that lie between 0 and 1, on the condition that they are not irrational numbers — because we want them to belong to our set of rational numbers. This restricts us to either terminating or infinitely repeating decimals, and prohibits us from using non-repeating decimals. Such a list might look like this:

$$\begin{aligned}
&\mathbf{0}.5000\\
&0.\mathbf{3}333\\
&0.4\mathbf{1}41\\
&0.66\mathbf{6}6\\
&0.250\mathbf{0}
\end{aligned}$$

Cantor's insight was to draw a diagonal line through this list as a means of selecting a new number. If we were to do so on the list above, we would get the number in bold, 0.3460..., which is clearly not among the original entries. Moreover, it can *never* be among the original entries, no matter how many new numbers we add to the grid. You could argue that it's possible to add only new numbers with lots of zeroes at the end, turning 0.3460... into 0.34600000 once and for all. But if you're committed to enumerating rational numbers, then at a certain point you'll have to add numerals greater than zero to the decimal places of your new numbers. If, on the other hand, you try to prove that your new number belongs to the rational numbers by putting it *in* the list, you will only create a new diagonal number. So you've demonstrated that the real numbers are greater than the rational numbers![11]

Some mathematicians still hold out on the diagonal argument, on the grounds that you never actually construct your real number, you've only "pointed to it." Our case is different, however, because we have the opportunity to verify it for ourselves,

[11] For an explanation of Cantor's proof pitched to the non-mathematician, see *Cantor's Diagonal Argument: A Most Merry and Illustrated Explanation (With a Merry Theorem of Proof Theory Thrown In)*, http://www.coopertoons.com/education/diagonal/diagonalargument.html (accessed August 14, 2014).

in an actual embodied case. Returning to Alexander in front of the mirror, we see that he has generated a list of commands, the subsets of which are subcommands expressed as instances in time. If we assign letters to these subcommands, a highly simplified list might look something like this at first:

t_0	t_1	t_2	t_3	t_4	t_5	t_6	t_7
o	a	a	a	a	a	a	speak#
o	b	b	b	b	b	b	lift arm#
o	a	b	a	b	a	b	speak while lifting arm#
o	a	b	c	a	b	c	sing while lifting arm#

Note that the subsets could be completely different from those I've drawn up here. Certainly, the actual subcommands involved in speaking, arm lifting and singing are a great deal more complex than I have presented them. Their complexity isn't relevant to the point, however. What matters is that they're countable. Each horizontal series of letters, while no longer strictly a number, nevertheless follows the same rule — once action commences, *if* action commences — of being either a terminal series or a repeating series. This means that the commands are recognizable as what I have been calling types.

So everything is built up into a perfect, unmoving block of defeat. But look what happens if we take away the zeroes at t_0:

t_0	t_1	t_2	t_3	t_4	t_5	t_6	t_7
b	a	a	a	a	a	a	speak#
b	b	b	b	b	b	b	lift arm#
b	a	b	a	b	a	b	speak while lifting arm#
b	a	b	c	a	b	c	sing while lifting arm#

Obviously, we've added a new command to the list to reflect whatever Alexander is doing at t0, which as given here is the vertical subset at to of {a, b, b, b}… *but without its negations* (because it's already taking place). This accomplished, everything comes together quickly. We see that a new line can be traced diagonally, or even haphazardly, *between* the proposed actions, and that this line, as in Cantor's argument, will be not appear in the set of rational numbers. At the same time, we can see that the empty set will not appear in the set, either, which, as we know from equivalence to the axiom of choice, means that there will be a choice function. In effect, Alexander has cornered himself, leaving no way out except for an uncountable course that cannot be constructed by the declarative mind. Therefore, something *else* must have used the axiom of choice. And because this something else does not name itself, the ban on self-belonging is not violated, and the circularity of foundation is broken.

This outcome is what set theorists call an independence result — in this case, rendering the axiom of replacement in one model (accomplished by introducing the monotype into each subset) and the axiom of choice in the other (choosing from the real numbers with the empty set removed). Since Alexander started with the idea of admitting the axiom of choice, by concerning himself with pre-existing sets as they came to his awareness, and ended up with its application independent of the original set (some agency selected a set that was never — and can never be — presented to him), he has demonstrated a distinct entity in his body without, as Russell put it, the need arising to describe it. Or, to paraphrase Tim Morton, who sees in the mesh of objects the encounter with a strange stranger, he has discovered the existence of a strange *companion*.

We had hoped to find as much when we began, and it turns out we got more than we expected. That there is an external ground for the axiom of choice in human activity is consistent with the findings of set theory. Where forcing usually deals with the ability to generate differences in set theory, here we see the forcing of a *different ground* for one of set theory's well-known axioms. This ability to shift between grounds, which by decentering the declarative mind certainly qualifies as a flat practice, lets another *being* use set theory according to the model at its disposal.

Interestingly, this procedure does not include *every* thought Alexander is able to think. If he were to include the thought of a zebra, any attempt to inhibit this thought would run into the familiar of puzzle of thinking it by trying not to think it. The class of action-commands is more clearly defined than "any thought whatsoever," and it's for this reason that the new set is able to avoid the problem of self-reference.[12] The execution of the action corresponding to the monotype # doesn't arise from the original set of actions — Alexander can't move his head up and forward while trying to speak just by declaring it to be possible — thus making it impossible for him to map his identity onto a set that includes this command.

It bears noting that this same command, while inaccessible to the personal identity, has been observed widely in the animal kingdom. Around the time Alexander was establishing himself, the scientist Rudolph Magnus established that, as a rule, mammals lead with the head when initiating an action.[13] Certainly my cat, which jumped away from my cup when I yelled incomprehensible words at her, led with her head. It also bears noting that the relation of the head and the neck, which Alexander called the primary control, determines *further* procedural decisions throughout the moving human body. That is, once the head is freed to move up and forward, the back is freed to widen

---

12 Bergson came within a hair's breadth of describing access to intuition through diagonalization: "By choosing images as dissimilar as possible, we shall prevent any one of them from usurping the place of the intuition it is intended to call up, since it would be driven away at once by its rivals. By providing that, in spite of their differences of aspect, they all require from the mind the same kind of attention, we shall gradually accustom consciousness to a particular and clearly defined disposition — that precisely which it must adopt in order to appear to itself as it really is, without any veil." Henri Bergson, "Introduction to Metaphysics," trans. T.E. Hulme (1903), 4–5, http://www.reasoned.org/dir/lit/int-meta.pdf (accessed February 27, 2015).

13 Rudolph Magnus, "Cameron Prize Lectures on Some Results of Studies in the Physiology of Posture," *The Lancet* (September 11, 1926): 531–36; and (September 18, 1926): 585–88.

in turn, and a general lengthening and decrease of tension progresses downward through the body. Free your neck, one might say, and the rest will follow. Within the domain of actions, the ability to move the head up and forward is *foundational* for the entire body with a brain in it, without ever being reducible to a command that I make directly. This is precisely the result that ooo seeks: the restitution of such a foundation to another virtual being, without appending to it the correlationist "I" that comes from unrestricted comprehension.

As mentioned, the Alexander Technique is often described in terms of mind–body unity. Dewey is notable in doing so, in keeping with his privileging of the unified whole in any kind of inquiry. I'm going to stick to my guns on this one, though. Alexander was describing his results within a historical context in which each body part was being considered separately of the others. In arguing for mind–body unity, the Alexandrian makes the case for a certain kind of supervenience: Every thought has a counterpart in the body. But the Alexandrian also claims the existence of two distinct modes of thought, one of which I am never able to access, but which can perform an action independent of my thought if I'm able to "stay out of my own way."[14] My argument leaves this claim intact, and gives Alexander's own claims greater clarity. On my view, the implicit mind withdraws from the brain and the body, giving *them* one unified negentropy, while the declarative mind has its *own* organizing influence that thinks of its local manifestation in parts. So much is evident from the fact that I begin by *not* thinking of my body as a whole, and as we have seen all along, by not being able to do so. If the relation of the head and neck is foundational for the entire human kinematic system, this is not the case for the *entire* human

14 It doesn't make it true, but at one point, Alexander very nearly comes out in favor of coincident entities: "[man] had thus been building up within himself two forces, as it were, until it was almost as if he had developed two separate entities. It was the conflicting demands of these 'separate entities' which [...] produced in him the condition of inward fear to which I refer." F. Matthias Alexander, *Constructive Conscious Control of the Individual* (Downey, CA: Centerline Press, 1985), 73.

being, because there *is* no entire human being. There are two beings at work in one body that never resolve into one.

In this respect, we need to take a closer look at the Alexandrian claim that the practice of his technique can establish improved use based on conscious control, since it suggests that the two agencies do gradually merge into one, and the logic of grounds forcing runs against this outcome. According to our set-theoretic reading, the repetition of a newly discovered action would mean moving a diagonalized series to a place among the horizontal series of actions. As we have seen, the result of such a move would merely be to create a new list, with a new diagonal. The real is simply pushed further out. Moreover, the original non-repeating diagonal will have been "rounded" to a rational number (as is trivially proven by it being repeatable), and so will lack some of its original content.

Alternatively, the recreation of the original diagonal might be accomplished by reducing the items on my list — that is, by limiting the complexity of my actions to those that obtained when I was able to force grounds the first time. (Remember, we can "disprove" diagonalization by reneging on our commitment to fill out the list of countable numbers.) This would entail repeating the conditions rather than the procedure, much as Kierkegaard did when he sought to recapture the magic of his adventure to Berlin.[15] Proceeding further in this direction, I might end up honing some technique of stillness removed from the clamor of life, but this quietude will prove difficult to maintain once I re-enter the world, where the list of imminent commands keeps changing. (In fact, the list will keep changing even in a monastery, for reasons I will take up in the following chapter.)

Fortunately, these theoretical predictions are borne out by the general observations of Alexander and his heirs alike. We can see the procedure is, strictly speaking, never completable,

---

15 Søren Kierkegaard, "Repetition: A Venture in Experimenting Psychology (October 16, 1843), by Constantin Constantius," in *The Essential Kierkegaard*, ed. Howard V. Hong and Edna H. Hong, (Princeton: Princeton University Press, 2000), 102–15.

because it produces actions that lie outside the enumerations of goals. That's what makes it a practice, or in Alexandrian terms, a means-whereby (which is also what prevents a whole being from ever appearing). As a related matter, the directions/inhibitions are held to be available in the midst of any activity. They are not, by any account of the Alexandrian project, related to any particular posture. They can be added into the normal course of affairs independently of those affairs — into whatever you happen to be doing at the time. To be more precise, {#} can be introduced into an infinitude of proposed actions without the need for any other rule to exist within those actions, because it is independent of those rules.

But independence from rules is a peculiar thing. Indeed, while grounds forcing might seem to invite comparison to Badiou's notion of forcing an event, it differs, as we had expected, by lacking the ingredients for Badiouan fidelity. Faithful to what? The opportunity for forcing is everywhere, across the constant opportunity to engage it or not. No name grants the right to claim that it is necessary. On the contrary, if one were to make "head up and forward" the proposed action itself, the entire enterprise would break down, since there would no longer be a command to place outside the proposed action. Alexander teachers counsel against overzealous use of the directions for this very reason. As defined, they're radically contingent: They only succeed because they fail to rise to the level of necessity. This is yet another reason for rejecting the thesis of a unified whole: As soon as you place the directions directly under your will, they stop working.

In this sense, grounds forcing is more in line with Meillassoux's cosmological view. As mentioned previously, Meillassoux argues that everything in the universe is contingent, that the only absolute is contingency itself. In the hyperchaos that is eternity, the outcome of stability is just as likely as is that of change, and physics becomes a temporally based investigation — a chronics. Grounds forcing affirms this chronics at the level of thought, or rather, literally, as a way of thinking that itself exists contingently. I don't get the promise of the One on the other side of my leap of faith. Because the reals defy typification, I enter a mesh of unknown outcomes. Or, as well: I arrive at an outer model for choice, at the gates of substitutive thought, where the mind blinks at the world beyond itself.

So, one might ask: Why bother doing it?

The short answer is: why not? But there are longer — and less flippant — answers, too.

For starters, there is the benefit of logical consistency within the framework of object-oriented ontology: The direction/inhibition method, which we might rechristen as the *primary decontrol,* systematically insures that its stimuli are linguistically defined, and then, having accumulated them in scrupulous array, forces them to allow a non-linguistic being to act in a clearly observable manner — without the declarative mind ever knowing what this other being perceives. Everything about the correlationist challenge militates against this possibility. And since we see that it *is* possible, and we can explain its mechanism, grounds forcing amounts to a demonstrated case of the human object entering into the multiplicity of objects, all of which exist on an equal footing.

That's a pretty good reason to endorse colocationism. Still, the possible is not the actual, and it's not so easy to see *how* one practices the procedure at the level of contingency it indicates. Obviously, most people don't take up the Alexander Technique because it's radically contingent. They come to it because their back hurts, or they have carpal tunnel syndrome, or they've heard that it's a technique for… stress reduction. Like its originator, they're drawn to it because of a problem. Given this, I might well wonder if I can truly have no special concern about its effect. Wouldn't its undertaking be motivated by the time-honored good of minimizing pain? And if so, what can it mean that the direct attempt to achieve any goal, even *this* goal, is precluded?

Where it seemed to be our friend, infinity now puts us in a hard spot, because the person with the problem apparently has to forget the reason for embarking on its solution *forever,* and this hardly seems likely to lead to an act of volition. If I'm to maintain the ontology of grounds forcing as I have defined it, I'm apparently led to conclude that the attainment of the good is simply not necessary. But this doesn't mean I should reject it. Most ethical theories are concerned with the negative consequences implied by a lack of control, disregarding that *trust* has a moral value. In this case, I've been given reason to believe that a certain procedure will result in the good, just not in a way I can predict, because it involves other objects and so does not lie entirely in my control. In fact, I have reason to believe that relinquishing the ideal of complete control over my motor skills is a condition *for* the attainment of the good.

This break in declared causality, as given by the value of trust, dovetails with the theory of ethics to which many Alexandrians would probably subscribe if presented with the options. Virtue ethics, once associated largely with Aristotle[16] and reinvigorated in recent years starting with G.E.M. Anscombe,[17] holds that the development of good habits, or a way of being, will lead to a flourishing, or *eudemonia,* which in turn will result in right actions. Learn to live a life of moderation, says Aristotle, and the good will follow. Similarly, practice the directions without undue zeal, and things will get better in general, without any great need to predetermine how.

The Alexandrian follows the idea of *eudemonia* closely, in that reasonable habit is expected to bring the good life about of its own accord. The efficacy of the method also gives it some bragging rights over duty-based, or deontological, theories of ethics, which aim for a set of rules that can be applied directly to actions. Certainly, a thought process that recognizes *only* means

---

16 Aristotle, *Nichomachean Ethics,* trans. F.H. Peters (New York: Barnes & Noble, 2005).
17 G.E.M. Anscombe, "Modern Moral Philosophy," *Philosophy* 33.124 (January 1958): 1–16.

and *no* ends will fly right past Kant's rule that another human should not be treated as merely a means to *an* end.[18] On the other hand, Alexander's approach (and any virtue ethics, for that matter) can be interpreted as duty-based, since it puts forward a rule — and in this case a rather heavily articulated one at that — which must be followed if the good life is to ensue. If we're not supposed to make its practice a duty, it then becomes a duty not to be dutiful, which looks like an evasion.

The difficulty points to the distinction between a motion and an action. In Aristotelian terms, we would like to disconnect the final cause of an action (its purpose) from its efficient cause (its agent), but find it hard to do so. And in fact, it's also hard to isolate the formal cause, which I have been calling a type, from some minimal reason for bringing it to fruition. After all, the response from my implicit mind, its free departure from reportable activity, isn't the end of the story, because the diagonal doesn't *remain* free. If I force the grounds of my action, I probably won't start singing opera while my cat looks on in arch bemusement. I probably will manage nonetheless to yell, "watch out," and pick up the cup. Nor is this an exceptional case: Success in achieving ends remains a part of the everyday life, even for the most devout practitioner of the means-whereby. Whenever I reach a declared goal *after* I've forced the grounds of my actions, then, the forcing procedure must have been shut down, at least for long enough to know what a cup is. And since we have supposed that knowing what a cup is requires a consistent personal identity, my success in achieving my goal gives strength to the argument that my experience of the cup is still correlated at any level that matters. As a bridge operator, the primary decontrol does not escape some degree of construction on the part of my declarative mind. Moreover, if I force the grounds of my action while reaching for the cup, and I inadvertently happen to treat another human as a means along the way (say, by accidentally stepping on my son's foot) and it then turns out that I do have an

---

18 Immanuel Kant, *Groundwork of the Metaphysic of Morals*, trans. H.P. Patton (New York: Harper & Row, 1964), 100–2.

end, I have apparently treated another human as a means to an end, which violates a reasonable standard for behaving ethically. The question as to whether I routinely treat my son *merely* as a means will then be open for debate, no doubt in relation to the value of the papers I rescued with my action.

Presented with this argument, I'm not left empty-handed. I can concede the point that life necessarily involves ends and reply that, by the same token, the diagonal can be reasserted as well. To give the reins over to another entity and then take them back in an ongoing two-step is, in a straightforward sense, simply what is meant by collaboration. The aim of equality with other entities, when formulated as a matter of trust, should not be to disable the declarative mind altogether, only to deny it the status of sole dominion.

Still, one is left with the feeling that the choice of *when* to return to the world of necessity is not a free one. There seems to be an end-based rule for returning to the rules, and this leads us back to the circular objection, because the end is already supposed prior to the action. I might try to overcome this difficulty by arguing that grounds forcing simply anticipates the inevitable reappearance of self-belonging. If, as in the case of Alexander, the problem is an inability to speak, and the solution is to regain this ability, it's nevertheless also the case that speaking becomes a means to a means, in an endless series, as new problems emerge. The elimination of one problem is not expected to vanquish *every* problem. Instead, it sets in motion a thought procedure in which personal identity is no longer necessarily defined by a *single* problem.

This approach, essentially the pragmatist's solution, distinguishes itself from moral relativism by posing grounds forcing as a series of experiments, any of which can be revised as the results become evident. I don't have to choose a problem. I can proceed with full confidence that one will always be waiting for me, right around the bend. The crucial point is that I learn from each inquiry and build from one to the next. However, it's easy to see that the pragmatic argument leaves the circular objection untouched. In the parlance of colocationism, it doesn't resolve the self-belonging of the master predicate under which the motivation for grounds forcing takes place. If my personal identity is defined by a series of problems, then I'm apparently made up of a series of personal identities connected by quasi-memories, as some writers have suggested.[19] Is this series one declarative mind? If so, we return to the original problem. If not, and I do learn progressively from my practice, then I will have to explain how these disconnected solutions come to be defined as progress. Progress according to what?

Indeed, a certain passivity is consistent with my original assumption. I held that the stimulus, though subject to negation, was nonetheless taken "as is." This in turn was to assume that the stimulus, though it formed in my mind as a declarative thought, originally came from somewhere else — that something besides *either* of my presumed entities determined what my options were. As the writers Velleman and George put it in their *Philosophies of Mathematics*: "It might help to think of choice sequences as a sequence of rational numbers that is generated by someone else."[20] I don't get to choose my choices — I inherit them. The diagonalization begins with actions that present themselves as necessary and moves *toward* their contingency. But I wasn't the one to construct the list in the first place, and I may feel that some aspects of it are unreasonable, or — just as important — someone else might feel that my list contains an element of privilege. It might be easier to decenter myself if, for example, I'm torn between a drive through the hills and another decanter of wine, as opposed to sweating under a restaurant kitchen hood and quitting.

Alexander leaves such considerations largely unanswered. In identifying a procedure that can be invoked in any circumstance, he declares a kind of scientific neutrality as to the external factors involved in any specific activity. His outlook is

---

19 Sydney Shoemaker, "Persons and Their Pasts," *American Philosophical Quarterly* 7.4 (October 1970): 269–85.

20 Alexander George and Daniel J. Velleman, *Philosophies of Mathematics* (Malden/Oxford: Blackburn, 2002), 136.

almost phenomenological, absorbed as he is with responding to the next presentation. This identification with imminent motor activity grants him a constant domain in which to proceed, yet the very same constancy leaves him open to charges of quietism, or at least to the perils of moral hazard: To practice his technique could be simply to allow the madness of life to wax madder. If I have a terrible taskmaster, so be it. If my *neighbor* has a terrible taskmaster, so be it. After all, no matter how grim the environment, I can always turn to the directions.

Alexander's discovery does not deliver a full-fledged ethics, even when distilled into set-theoretic form. He did, however, develop a makeshift evolutionary theory that gives us a clue as to how to proceed. As he lays it out in *Conscious Control of the Individual*,[21] early humans were well adapted to their environment, but our own powers of reason have made it increasingly inhospitable. Today, an act as simple as sitting in a chair, evidently built by a rational animal, imposes a set of demands that tax the instincts, because it's fundamentally foreign to the instincts. Multiply the circumstances of the chair by all the "foreign" objects one encounters in a lifetime, and the result is a global collapse of the body, as instinct is overwhelmed by an unforgiving habitat.

Tellingly, when Alexander takes on the cause of this collapse, he traces it not so much to objects *per se* as to objects we *make*. He's concerned not with volcanoes or puddles, but with golf clubs and chairs. It's only because we make things, words and wicker baskets alike, that we're presented with commands that exceed our instincts. So much is at least consistent with our ethical concern about the context in which actions take place,

---

[21] While Alexander identifies civilization with an artificial environment throughout his writings, he addresses it specifically within the context of human evolution in the first chapter of this book. For example: "as the pathway of [man's] experience inevitably widened out, he was confronted with one of the greatest difficulties experienced in his evolutionary progress [...] that of adapting himself quickly to an environment which continued to change with ever-increasing rapidity." Alexander, *Constructive Conscious Control of the Individual*, 46.

since it's difficult to imagine a human motor activity that's not related in *some* way to an object of human manufacture. For a counterfactual example, eliminate clothes, then every other cultural artifact in the environment, one by one, and Mark Twain's insight becomes obvious: The naked man has little or nothing to say about society. It seems well within reason, then, to consider grounds forcing, not only in terms of the production of language, as was Alexander's goal before the mirror, but also as it devolves onto garden variety objects such as cups and chairs.

This line of thought leads us to a mode of practice advocated by Ian Bogost. In *Alien Phenomenology*,[22] Bogost proposes that we direct philosophy, so often tethered to the written word, toward the creation of physical artifacts that illustrate how objects construct their own worlds, a practice he calls *carpentry*. Different kinds of objects, by his lights, affect our thoughts according to rules unique to their construction.

I agree with Bogost that objects can present their own worlds to us, or — to put it in the terminology now in bloom — that they can exhibit to me some foundation of their own. It seems, too, that the ability to decenter my own *grounds* for decentering myself must lie at least partly with the grounds of other things. My interest going forward, accordingly, will be to extend the principle of grounds forcing into carpentry — to orient an object within a context in such a way as to diagonalize my relation to it.

My reservations about this adventure have only to do with its threshold for success. Unlike Bogost, who advocates as light an ontology as possible, I'm committed to coincidence, which places a heavy restriction on what qualifies as news from an object on its own terms. On one hand, Alexander makes a convincing case that *any* artifact will qualify as carpentry if I'm able to decenter my coincident entities, one from the other. Through the procedure of grounds forcing, I can discover the world that objects present. But I've also found that the being of every object

---

22 Ian Bogost, *Alien Phenomenology, or What It's Like to Be a Thing* (Minneapolis: University of Minnesota Press, 2012).

vanishes in the rush of ends that inadvertently belong to me. Ironically, this seems especially so when it comes to a thing I make, because I don't make the whole world. I only make this or that object, and when I look for a value by which to choose the production of one object over another, grounds forcing does not provide one. As Graham Harman has asked in much the same vein: "is there any way to avoid an endless repetition of the insight that all reality swings between a concealed and a revealed mode? Is there any way to gain even a few insights into how each *metabole* in reality is different from the others?"[23]

To which we might add, just to keep things interesting, can we gain these insights from within the colocationist argument itself?

---

23 Graham Harman, "A Fresh Look at Zuhandenheit (1999)," in *Towards Speculative Realism* (Winchester & Washington, DC: Zero Books, 2010), 66.

4

Personal Effects

After I established these things, I thought I was entering port; but when I began to meditate about the union of soul and body, I felt as if I were thrown again into the open sea. For I could not find any way of explaining how the body makes anything happen in the soul, or vice versa, or how one substance can communicate with another created substance. Descartes had given up the game at this point, as far as we can determine from his writings.
— Leibniz[1]

In the previous chapter, we saw how predicated thoughts could, by an indirect method, force motions that exceed predication. But what about direct commands? How do explicit thoughts result in recognizable actions? If I think, "Pick up the cup," how does this arrangement of words translate into the motions in my arm, my hand, my feet, such that the action conforms, even approximately, to the thought? Leibniz couches the question in terms of the soul, but the mystery remains even when Cartesian dualism is discounted: How does a thought translate into a motion?

At this point, we're at least able to understand why there *is* a question. For a local manifestation with only one virtual being (assuming such a manifestation exists), the translation of thought into motion would have no remainder, and the problem would never even come up for contemplation. A being with

---

1   Gottfried Wilhelm Leibniz, "A New System of Nature," *Philosophical Essays*, ed. Roger Ariew and Daniel Garber (Indianapolis: Hackett Publishing Company, 1989), 143.

a one-to-one match between mind and body would live like a born Zen master, without so much as a path between here and *satori*. The question itself—"how does thought translate into motion?"—is only there to be asked because the implicit mind is not alone in the body.

This explanation does not get us very far, though. For one thing, it still says nothing about how *any* kind of thinking ends up as doing, and yet, for all that, one has to admit that the doing gets done. If I'm unable to understand the mechanism of activity from within my own perspective, I simply fob off the work of that mechanism onto my other thinker, even though *I* was the one to think, "Pick up the cup." And I've strongly implied that my other thinker doesn't know the meaning of words, which makes fulfillment of the command puzzling, to the say the least.

We began to get some purchase on the problem when we identified speech as a threat to the implicit mind. An action that carries a meaning for me—the production of syllables in syntactic combination—prompts a response that has no relation to the semantic content of those syllables. My implicit mind doesn't respond to truth statements with a keen grasp of their subtleties. It's startled by clear propositions the same as it is by foolish lies. So language does cause some kind of physical response, even if it's not the response actually being requested. Given the ubiquity of speech, we can also surmise that this threat must be more than momentary, and the startle response more or less a constant of the human condition. If this is so, as the studies of Frank Pierce Jones and others indicate, then we get a perplexing result: The dangerousness of speech cannot be specifically named, because the danger is conveyed by speech *per se*, and, moreover, the broadcast of any other danger (say, the imminent approach of a flood) will be compromised by a fear of the message. As a result, a basic purpose of signals—to report a threat as the motivation for an action—is rendered unreliable.

This unreliability is a stumbling block for many explanations of how language emerged, and the challenge certainly applies to my case as well. The cost of living in fear—worse, being unable to identify the reason for it—appears to be inordinately high.

Alexander gets around this objection by making the negative consequences of civilization, including language, so gradual that they go unnoticed until it's too late. On my view, however, there is a stronger explanation — stronger because it works whether the development of language is fast or slow, yet preserves both the high price of unreliable signals and their flowering nonetheless.

As we have seen, speech can't be easily reduced to the efficient workings of instinct — or, to maintain the terminology I've borrowed from Bryant, the negentropy of the implicit mind. When I talk, I'm engaged in an activity that my implicit mind perceives as a foreign intrusion. But as it does so, it also goes into a startle, which in turn changes the mechanics of speaking. There may be two minds, but there's still only one body. So if the question "how does thought cause motion?" itself implies thoughts that are not strictly in accord with the negentropy of the implicit mind, we might suppose that these "extra" thoughts also cause motions in excess of the *motions* that would occur if only the implicit mind were present.

Let's suppose, a little brazenly, that this is true: The overcrowded human simply displaces or donates its overcrowdedness to its local manifestation. (One can see the stirrings of this hypothesis in Leibniz, who, in his *New System of Nature*, redirects Descartes' question "what conserves me?" from bodily organs to bodily motion.) Such a proposition might seem unwarranted from the start because, although the declarative and implicit minds are clearly not manifestations, I nonetheless have granted them *quantity* insofar as I've admitted that there are two of them. It may seem, then, that I've granted mathematical operators the status of objects that occupy space. This isn't necessarily the case, however.

A case in point is the estuary we considered earlier. As a body of water that's part ocean and part river, an estuary is subject to both tides and currents, and is characterized by brackish water and a distinct ecozone. Most people would happily grant that water takes up space, but tides and currents are a different matter. Each of these forces is distinct, yet they mingle in the same material. There is no place in the estuary where either force is absent. On the contrary, their mutual presence defines the boundaries of the estuary. While a human being is clearly not an estuary, the reasoning is much the same: It's not at all clear that mathematical operators have any dimensionality of their own, and the burden of proof lies with those who would argue that they do. Hence the argument for colocation, at least as presented so far, does not require us to accord spatial dimension to thought.

But we can't leave space out of our equation entirely. Even if the initial thought of a sentence retains its weird nowhereness, we would be remiss to think that the resulting *motions* of speech obey anything but ordinary physical laws. And motions, as we know, are translated from one object to another. What this will mean for a coinhabited body is the appearance of extraneous motion — first in the body itself, and then in its contiguous environment. As with the combined forces of tide and current, which act on the banks to create unique effects, speech will extend beyond the limits of the body as an air flow that's the product of two sources of propagation, and therefore somehow already a different kind of signal than a straightforward animal call.

Nor is there any reason to suppose that this effect should be limited to speech. The irrepressible fidgeting of children — let it be their polymorphous perversity — is well known to the long-suffering parent. Excess motion can come out of one part of the body or another, or from many parts at once, for no reason except that it has to come out.[2] Needless to say, these motions will also extend to objects in the environment and alter them, just as speech does — indeed, all the more vividly when a denser object receives the impact. The difference between a wave traveling through the air and a scratch etched in granite is one of degree only. So it seems reasonable to suppose that coincidence in humans entails marking the world, literally, in a way that's

[2] Bryant has made a similar connection between the polymorphously perverse and natural selection. Levi Bryant. "Polymorphously Perverse Nature," *Larval Subjects*, August 17, 2013, http://larvalsubjects.wordpress.com/2013/08/17/polymorphously-perverse-nature/ (accessed August 15, 2016).

not reducible to a single agent. Let's call this progression, with more attention to geometry than to lumens, *radiance,* and its point of inertia, where friction brings a halt to the impulse, a *personal effect.*

Now everything is turned around. We've been assuming that the pursuit of a goal relies on the formulation of that goal in advance. Radiance, however, implies that personal effects are *existential* in the narrow sense of the term: They exist before they have essence. A motion born of multiple causes will, by its very multiplicity, lack any grounds for its execution, and so too its target: The end will appear without aforethought. On the colocationist view, the high price of cultural artifacts is paid whether we like it or not, and intelligence itself is put on the defensive, because personal effects develop haphazardly, out of the *accidents* of an unmastered body.

Lucretius famously attributed novelty in the universe to the *clinamen,* or swerve, which affected atoms unpredictably in their downward fall through the void.[3] Here I'm proposing a specific variant of the swerve as a consequence of colocation, making no claims about the existence of the same principle elsewhere in the universe, while nevertheless maintaining that its novel effects arise without any fixed rule other than the rules of physics (which, according to Lucretius, may change as well). Artifacts appear prior to any immediately obvious functions. We're artists and inventors first, reckoners later.

Of course, this swerve will be devilishly hard to witness, because we're in it. Some readers will have had the experience of holding a spinning bicycle wheel and feeling an unexpected spiraling pull to the side. After several goes at it, the gyroscopic effect loses the element of surprise and one adjusts. Now, if a similar force were at work in our bodies at all times, we would compensate from the first throes of consciousness and never necessarily know that we were doing so. Moreover, because in our case both forces are withdrawn from the same body, as op-

---

3   Lucretius, *On the Nature of Things,* trans. Frank O. Copley (New York: W.W. Norton, 1977), 34.

posed to one of them being withdrawn from the wheel, their multiple volitions would radiate as one effect — *a vector* — as they're forced through the bottleneck of a single manifestation.

What begins to emerge, then, is an explanation for extension that manages to retain a Cartesian flavor. Overcrowding causes a co-dependent motion, which creates radiant effects on objects outside the body, but only when the declarative mind is active. Every *conscious* perception thus meets up with its already-embarked effect on the world. Because these imprints of thought saturate experience, it never appears as if anything is amiss. It seems that this is how the world looks.

That looks like a neatly locked up argument. But there's also a strange assumption in it. I've said that my declarative and implicit minds can contribute to a novel effect by virtue of exerting themselves simultaneously, and also that my participation in the creation of that effect eludes my explicit awareness of it. In other words, a conscious thought causes an effect of which it remains unaware — even as it is causing it. How can this be?

The answer, I believe, can be found if we hark back to the explicit model. The declarative mind cannot resolve the gaps in its self-evident existence. I think, therefore I am, and when I do not think, I apparently am not. Because it is the case that I think intermittently, I'm unable to traverse an action without inventing a bridge operator, some other declarative mind to which I attach my identity. That's what I've claimed so far. Now it appears that when I do think, the very existence of my conscious thought changes my environment, even in broad daylight. The suggestion, then, is that the change occurs in the gap. I do before I perceive what I do, just because the implicit mind and I both exist. Yet I never encounter the *perspective* of the implicit mind. I encounter a fabricated being to which I have inevitably assigned attributes of a perspective that is not mine but is inevitably *like* mine, since I participate in its construction.

How this plays out becomes a little clearer if we consider awareness in terms of space as well as time. If, for example, I hold my attention on some *remote* object — say, a star — my gaze will obviously do nothing to alter the star, but my body will continue marking the world around me nonetheless.[4] That this activity occurs while I'm fixating on some distant object must mean that I'm not paying attention to everything I'm doing, and therefore beginning to generate *abstract* effects. To borrow from Saussure, we could say that such effects are unmotivated, in that they conform neither to the execution of instinct (not completely, anyway) nor directly to the object of which I am aware. To build on Lacan, we could go further and say that the unconscious is structured like a language — with a crucial disclaimer: My unconscious, at least my waking unconscious, is not inside me, awaiting my curious introspection. It's on the outside. What fills the gap is in the world.[5]

As it stands, the description is no doubt simplistic. The scenario I'm painting suggests a narrowing down to a focal point, and on request we're generally able to achieve something better than tunnel vision.[6] By the same token, I don't mean to suggest that we generate waking dreams in our peripheral vision (although that might be pleasant). The effect can be as fine-grained as attention allows. If we follow a Wittgensteinian model, in which our picture of the world is subject to higher and higher resolutions, the reportable result will never manage to provide a complete representation.[7] But to this model, which is supposed to lead us to reject what cannot be pictured, we can add not only subliminal motor activity — as we investigated with the help of cup and cat — but subliminal *production* as well. Around (or beside or interspersed within) the view I have before me, my own unmotivated activities begin to accrue, with no particular destination in mind.

---

4 It's worth remarking that Friedrich Besser, known for describing the principle of parallax, also took it upon himself to observe the inconsistent procedural motions of his colleagues as they peered through the telescope at stars, and so became the first to articulate what is known in the philosophy of science as the Personal Equation.
5 What sleeping dreams are made of is, sadly, beyond the scope of this essay.
6 Although Dennett says we don't. Dennett, *Consciousness Explained*, 53–54.
7 Ludwig Wittgenstein, *Tractatus Logico-Philosophicus,* trans. C.K. Ogden (New York: Barnes & Noble, 2003), 15–19.

If in promulgating this view, I've passed the point of no return for most philosophers of action, who take intention to have at least some minimal content preceding its execution, I can only say it's going to get worse.[8] The unmotivated nature of human activity, its existential restlessness, provides what I believe is an adequate explanation for creativity, which, after all, happens without direct intention every time. It also gives us the framework for understanding how instinct can come to be compromised. But the consequences go further, because strictly speaking, unmotivated dislocations of the kind I'm describing should arise whenever I'm paying attention to anything.

To return to language of the explicit model: Holding my attention on a star is the same operation as generating the star as a type. As I contemplate it and then renew my decision to do so, I confirm its sameness over time, which is to render my previous impression of it identical in some way to its current status, even if I notice a glint of red that I missed a moment ago. I establish the star as an identity that persists across its variations. This is exactly the bare-bones employment of the axiom schema of replacement. Meanwhile, my personal effects are already coming to be, unthematized as yet and governed only by the limits that the world provides. They may show some preponderance toward utterances, for the simple reason that oxygen is always there. Maybe I start to hum. Or, if I stand long enough in that pleasantly uncomfortable position of stargazing, I begin to scuff the ground in a distinctive way. Then my attention shifts — to a rustle in the woods — and the dislocation continues.

Here's the point where Pandora herself might have balked. If I now direct my attention to the marks on the ground, I'm repeating the retention process and inducing another dislocation, which in turn causes yet another dislocation, and so on. Every time I hold my attention on anything — by virtue of the

---

[8] Bratman goes so far as to claim that intentions are already in progress with the formulation of a plan. I'm claiming that an action is in progress before the intention even arises. Michael Bratman, *Intention, Plans, and Practical Reason* (Cambridge, MA: Harvard University Press, 1987).

simple fact that "I" am a mathematical operator who employs the axiom of replacement—I'm furthering a chain of types in tandem with a chain of dislocations: two chains, which may or may not have any relation to each other. In the previous chapter, I promised to explain why a list of actions staged for diagonalization will keep changing, and this is it. Coincidence perpetually rearranges its own habitat.

In making the connection between unmotivated activity and the unassigned object, we've reconciled Alexander's theory of evolution with colocationism. The overcrowding of our minds leads to novel motions and, for reasons that turn out to be almost mechanical, novel manifestations, which make their own demands on us in turn. Naturally (I say naturally because I consider my account of productivity to be suitably naturalized at this point), these demands begin without a predetermined destiny, and could become tools or signs, or all manner of disaster and clutter.

This is still only half the battle, though. Despite the headway we've made, our coincident entities still communicate not by direct address, but through an almost comic slippage from memory to motion, and this doesn't seem like a recipe for quality control. Unmotivated activity may be adequate for the production of strange things hitherto unseen, but it's hard to imagine that the same could hold true for reproduction. To return to our original question, then, how does a goal, once recognizable as such, come to be accomplished?

While we can't peer back in time to observe the moment the first entity had the first pre-meditated intention, we can approach this question, using an old trick from the transcendental repertoire, by asking another one: Under what conditions *could* a chain of intention be initiated? How would radiance turn out to generate results *besides* disaster and clutter?

Suppose again that I look at a star and, as a result, absentmindedly create a design in the dust that's sufficiently strange to attract my curiosity. This attraction alone means that I turn my attention to the design. By the same principle we're supposing, the very act of beholding the design, of typifying it, would initiate another dislocated motion. But notice that, unlike the star, the design in the dust *is* within my means to alter. Suppose further then, that I do *not* alter the design, but instead continue to gaze at it. I *can* touch it, but I do not. All that's needed now is to prolong this decision and the object will be defined by the rule "do not touch." This, of course, is an object familiar to anthropologists of every stripe — an object that's set apart, kept separate: a *sacred* object. In keeping with Meillassoux's etymology, which traces "absolute" to its meaning of "severance,"[9] I propose to call such an entity an *absolute object*.

An absolute object doesn't satisfy a positive definition of intention, in the sense of "I intend x," but it does pretty well as a double negative. "Given x, I intend not not-x." (Or, as it's written in logical notation, $\sim\sim x$, where a tilde means "not.") Absolute status is simply a projection of the sameness of an object over time, with the presumption of some control over its endurance. By the rules of transcendental analysis, we're unable to ascribe a motive for the decision in favor of this restraint. It's plain enough, though, that the condition holds good for the advent of a great experiment in controlling the environment. Whatever the reason not to touch what I can touch, the sequence will proceed as it did when I gazed at the star, in a contagion of effects, except that I can now refuse or agree to act on a multitude of secondary effects as they spring up before me. Far from being deliberate, then, my intentions will be more like an absorption in the properties of the things, with absolute objects providing stable points of reference. If I bar myself from coming in contact with some personal effect, will it be demolished by other forces anyway? And if it is demolished, will that be something I "did?" Are there other effects I can continue to touch without fear of changing them — that I might, on the contrary, try to demolish and find still intact? Can I reconstitute an effect after it falls to decay, and if so, where is it located then — in my memory, or in the thing? If it exists in my memory, how can I stabilize *that*? *Can* I stabilize that?

---

9   Meillassoux, *After Finitude*, 28.

The propulsive nature of radiance keeps these questions from being merely academic. They're posed to a body moving among other objects. This means that the condition of the absolute object is able to provoke *imminent* questions about intentions, the answers to which will constitute a material culture and its associated values. Over time, we could in fact expect an accumulation of intentional "pathways," along which the next implied step would tend to be occupied by a conventional expectation. What we call mastery would then be the statistically accurate *save* of the next implied effect, while the swerve would be any divergence from this expected next type, due to the participation of two agencies in the task.

At this point, we might have a hunch where all this is going. The constant throughout the chain seems to be my personal identity, so the temptation is to fall in with Aristotle — and Kant — and award this constant the position of final cause, or in the Kantian formulation, the rational being as an end in itself. Yet the free variable, for which there is no account, is my decision to hold my attention or, just as unaccountably, to shift it. Since this decision starts the intentional chain, it occurs prior to any entity that could make it, including the persistence of me as I understand as myself. My personal identity arises *with* my decision to typify an object and therefore cannot be enlisted as the agent choosing in favor of holding my attention on *that* object. By extension, the same holds for choosing which dislocation I save and which I allow to slip into the new: I'm unable to ground this choice on an enduring personal identity.

Our account of intention now folds in with our account of coincident entities, point by point, and even gives us a little boost, because it allows us to consider productivity in terms of grounds forcing and carpentry.

With the primary decontrol, the basic procedure was to refuse to respond to a set of intended actions. Here again we see a refusal as crucial to the process, but now the refusal itself, the refusal to cause a change in x, is an intention. Not only that, but the refusal to cause a change in x is, on some stupid but clearcut level, a means of ensuring my independence from another entity. Further, if I refuse to cause a change in x that is within my power to change, then my radiance will necessarily be diverted elsewhere. So it looks like extended grounds forcing should be a mirror image of the Alexandrian procedure. Rather than assert one impossible action and refuse everything else, I refuse only one possible action and consent to the surprising world that follows.

This may seem to present yet another contradiction. How, one might ask, can I simultaneously refuse and consent to the same class of activities? Surely, this is a classic example of the excluded middle, which requires me to choose either to decontrol my actions or to separate myself from some object. But in fact, no choice is necessary, because diagonalization worked in the former case by refusing everything within a limited class, thus forcing choice onto another operator, and the same shadow moves just as surely across the latter. It's no more possible to obey *every* command within a limited class that's presented to me than it is to follow none of them at all. On the contrary, far from contradicting each other, the combination of the two procedures brings out the very point we were hoping to be able to make.

As will be recalled, in thinking "head up and forward," we received every stimulus as it came and then forced the grounds of motor activity, until we returned by some unknown formula to an intention. But this return can never be a return to *every* intention. Something has to be left as not done. And this must be true whether we decenter our actions or not. There's always something that we don't do at the expense of what we do. So what we're attempting now, really, is to give reiterative power to "something not done," such that it's not simply the vast, undefined complement of what's intended, nor an ever-shifting pragmatic foundation for action, but something definitely not done that remains the same thing regardless of what *is* done. Basically, we're adding one action into each variation of the actions we might propose, and then refusing it along with the rest.

In our pursuit of this Archimedean point, we've gained another advantage along the way. We no longer have to worry about an original intention, because we no longer presume intentions to arise prior to effects. I enter into the task of separating an object with everything already at my disposal, and with my radiant proclivities already acting on my contiguous environment. This will be helpful, because — continuing to be a little dense about it — the only way to know that it's definitively within my power to cause a change to x is to *have* caused some change to it. And with this knowledge in hand, the next step will be clear: to refuse to cause some *further* change to x, because this knowledge will then also be knowledge of a thing that has the possibility of persisting without me.

The absolute object is therefore a curiously versatile thing. Normally, one thinks of an object that's set apart as an index for some other unseen entity. Here it warrants our interest strictly for its independence from us. In fact, rather than eliciting our veneration or offering a focal point for our deepest wishes, it actually defines the challenge, from within the ontology of coincident entities, for acting on an equal footing with other objects. The challenge, let's still call it my challenge, is this: to identify an existing class of personal effects, to alter some element x in that class such that it blocks every bridge operation for how x entails y, and then to withhold my ability to further alter that element in any way that reintroduces a bridge operator other than the effect itself. This plan remains within the orbit of a virtue ethics, because the idea is to set up a structure in which there is an absolute object, and then to see if it can have *no* limiting relation to any action I might take within that structure. I will want to stabilize an object only long enough to start it on its journey, not to control what happens next. The theory being, if I can sustain this pressure, intentions that do not *only* originate from within the correlationist circle will be freed to leap to the fore.

On one level, my task is starting to look almost easy now, since, according to the argument as it stands, I should be able to seize upon most any object and stop its becoming-for-me in midstream. In fact, I'm perilously close to a campaign for magical thinking, as if I could just carry a talisman around and expect the noumenal world to announce itself to me. What I have yet to address in this regard is a certain unnerving vulnerability that radiance provokes, a vulnerability that's closely tied up with the assertion of sameness for "something not done" — not sameness over time anymore, or rather, not only over time, but also across space. So we have one last stop to make before plunging into the wilderness of beings.

To restate the argument on the table: If my personal identity arises *with* the assignment of purpose to other objects, then it seems fair to say that those other objects will count in some respect as part of my identity. This view — that thought is conditional on the environment — is known as externalism, and it has the usual spectrum of positions. Those mining the Anglo-American vein may be reminded especially of the extended mind thesis, advanced by Clark and Chalmers, which holds that some objects actually do some of the thinking for us. A man named Otto, beset with Alzheimer's, uses his notebook to find his way to a museum. Otto does not actually have the knowledge of where the museum is located; therefore, the notebook does. Such is the example, highly condensed, that Clark and Chalmers put forward to argue that Otto and the notebook exhibit parity in their ability to think.

So much resonates nicely with the function of an external bridge operator as I described it earlier, only now the operator is not just imagined as existing outside the body — it actually *is* outside. Although an external fact, the notebook is still *part of* Otto's intention. He moves from one patch of awareness to the next, counting on it to maintain the structure of time and space for him. (Without getting too deeply into aesthetics, it's also certainly noteworthy that the authors chose a museum as the target location, given the Herculean efforts of museum staffs the world over to preserve the sameness of artworks over time.) With colocationism, we also get the benefit, thrown in for free, of explaining why there *are* such things as notebooks. The production of artifacts *per se* is an existential fact, as a matter of radiance, for as long as I'm blessed to have two minds. My thoughts are already pushed "out there," into things, before I can think them through. And in fact, an entire subgenre in the coincidence literature is devoted to these objects, which seem to be both statue and clay, road and pavement.

But Chalmers and Clark go further than the powers of workaday storage devices in their thesis. "And what," they ask, "about socially-extended cognition? Could my mental states be partly constituted by the states of other thinkers? We see no reason why not, in principle."[10] Indeed, why not? The notebook, after all, stores more than just the information that Otto has put in it. The inventors of the calendar and the alphabet, the manufacturers of the paper that makes up its pages, the worker who confirms that the pages are bound, the truck driver who delivers the shrink-wrapped skids of notebooks to the store... all of these parties have extended their minds into the object, and left a mark there before ebbing. Otto benefits from the survival of these thoughts as much as he does from his own inscriptions. On this view, civilization itself can be seen an exercise in people "thinking into" objects that exist in the great outdoors.

The colocationist will tend to accept the idea of socially extended cognition early on, since the implicit and declarative minds clearly rely on each other and, moreover, even seem to foreshadow a social sensibility. Having added the corollary of radiance, we now also have a means of engaging collective agency right and proper, not just as an interesting idea about Otherness entertained from the comfort of our own idealist thoughts, but as a disruption in our sincere endeavors when other people actually do show up.

Usually, the subject of collective agency is introduced with a decision, as if beginning from a blank slate. "Suppose a group of people decide to build a house..." Radiance counsels us to approach the matter from a different angle, however, because it entails that activities come first and intentions follow. I'm al-

---

10 Andy Clark and David Chalmers, "The Extended Mind," *Analysis* 58.1 (January 1998): 17.

ready in the midst of a welter of intentions, some of which are my own and some of which belong to others, before I take it into my head to start building a house. Normally, I'm not aware of this. It doesn't occur to me that others have been "thinking into" my activities, or I into theirs, so long as I can proceed with my own thoughts and activities. It's only when something goes awry that the chains of intentions become apparent to me. Here one immediately recalls Heidegger's hammer, which, when broken, reveals the truth undergirding the world. But this isn't where the argument is headed anymore. When my hammer breaks, it doesn't illuminate being. It reveals shoddy craftsmanship, and behind that, someone who wasn't thinking into the hammer for *me*.

This kind of unveiling can put socially extended cognition through some rigorous paces. Suppose I go to the hardware store to complain, pieces of a former tool in hand. To my surprise, the clerk just pops the head back on the handle and hands it back to me. "It isn't broken," says my service representative, quickly turning adversary. "You just have to reattach the head."

For the first time, I notice some kind of flanges on the handle that I've never associated with hammers before. And the head does *seem* to stay on. "But..." I stammer, "won't it just fall apart next time?" To which comes the reply: "It depends on how much force you use."

Ah, yes, how much force I use. The definition of "broken" has now become an annoying borderline case, in which our social extensions are actually mutually exclusive. I'm trying to implant an action in the clerk (to provide me with a new hammer), while the clerk is trying to implant a different action in me (to accept the original hammer and go away). There are two different chains of intentions that crossed once, briefly, and have proceeded onward to different ends. To put it another way, the hammer is part of two larger objects that are differently composed.

So much might be dismissed as a nuisance of modern life. But now suppose that I go home and start to work on my house again. Bang, bang, bang—I'm making solid progress on some renovations in my living room when swoop, off flies the hammerhead again, arcing across the room, and hitting... *my cat*. In fact, it catches him right in the temple as he jumps off my desk and kills him on the spot!

The consequences of multiple intentions suggested by this incident threaten to pour some fairly cold water on the project of decentering the human. If I accept the differing definitions of a working hammer, I accept a world broken into subjective parts, in which everyone interprets the hammer as they like and the hammer itself goes unseen, like the neglected child of divorce. Not only is this precisely the kind of misguided conversation that the OOO project strenuously seeks to avoid, it also seems to ask for a resolution, now that my cat is a casualty. Yet if I seek consensus on the definition of the hammer, I find no answer in the hammer, which, unlike my arms and legs, has no clear-cut place to which it belongs. As an extended mind, the hammer is, in a very real sense, *numb*. Its "hammerness" has no negentropy of its own. Sensation will be of little assistance to me here, because the hammer's hammerness exists only in its exo-relations, which the clerk and I have discovered to be less than congruent. If I reject the subjective position, then, the only obvious recourse is to petition some encompassing entity inside which our differing ends can be squared up. That is, some external agent the clerk and I invest with the power to render judgment about the persistence or change of an object over time — an arbiter to settle the case.

This kind of "for us," the judicial "for us," is probably desirable for most people, even those who seek to overcome correlationist "for us" on philosophical grounds.[11] We look to the voice that speaks "for us" to resolve the many squabbling "for me's," sometimes in cases as small-time as the definition of a tool, sometimes in cases with a lot more in the game. (Fill in the blank: "Jerusalem is the extended mind of ___.") Interestingly, the figure of arbiter as I conceive it yields more than a passing resemblance to Harman's idea of a vicar. According to

---

11 It's all but impossible to suppress the image here of André Breton convening his grand councils to determine who was a true Surrealist and who failed to make the grade.

Harman, the withdrawal of objects throughout the universe immediately leads the problem of how they can ever interact. His solution, which he calls vicarious causation, is to introduce an object — a vicar — that contains them both and so allows them to interact on its interior. Substitute "arbiter" for "vicar" and you get much the same result.[12] An arbiter can give a ruling that we both believe brings our intentions into relation with each other and therefore causes us to reconcile our conflicting compositions of the hammer. We will think the same thoughts into the hammer hereafter.

Or so the theory would have it. Of course, the arbitration system will run into familiar difficulties. I can probably find a serviceable candidate for my complaint, and if our arbiter gets entangled in the dispute, recusal from the case is presumably an option, but logically speaking there can be no *final* arbiter as to what *all* objects "really are," because eventually no more recusals will be available and the final arbiter will end up as one of those seeking arbitration.

It might be objected here that no final arbiter is needed, that a temporary arbiter could just as well arise for each occasion and each object in dispute, simply because there is no such thing as "all objects."[13] Yet we do encounter this figure of the final arbiter, generally coming forth with a pretense to extending its mind into every body in its dominion, in order to undertake *its* intentions (which should probably not surprise us, since personal effects are by their nature "loose" in the world). How this court of last resort plays out has been well tracked under the heading of structural agency. The judgment as to the status of personal effects can only be imparted through the medium of other personal effects, which are necessarily manifested locally, yet need to communicate a total domain. By this route, we end up with Althusser's policeman, who — on finding me conducting a

---

12 Graham Harman, "On Vicarious Causation," *Collapse* 2, ed. Robin Mackay (2007): 187–221.
13 While the medieval aspect of this solution is appealing, the arbiters for hammers are likely to find themselves at odds with the arbiters for nails soon enough, and to seek a larger union.

mock funeral for my cat outside the hardware store — hails me in the midst of my spectacle and *makes* me turn around, thereby constituting me as a subject of the state.[14] The policeman's uniform is the extended mind of the final arbiter and, in appearing from an unambiguously exterior vantage point, causes my double agency to fuse into a single subject, a coincident entity no more... an in-dividual.

In seeking a mathematical basis for coincident entities, we identified an anti-foundational maze within the declarative mind, and we met up with it again in the circularity of personal identity and manufactured object. Now, having expanded our inquiry to include other minds, we find it obstinately in force at the level of material culture *writ large*. Moreover, we've reached the point where the personal effect of the final arbiter, which we might call an *absolute personal effect,* brings together in lockstep the two forms of indifference to identification that I mentioned at the outset — indifference to the signifier and to the signified. The name of the effect now has no substitute, nor does the effect itself. Everything converges onto an exact expression of agency.

That's one way to solve the problem of causation within the sphere of human long-suffering striving. Strictly speaking, though, the finality of the final arbiter brings with it all the instability that comes with the prospect of self-belonging.[15] The shakiness of the contradiction will show up at the top, where power turns capricious with great regularity, and, because the totalization that provokes self-belonging is simply unattainable,[16] again

---

14 Louis Althusser, *On the Reproduction of Capitalism: Ideology and Ideological State Apparatuses,* trans. G.M. Goshgarian (London/New York: Verso, 2014), 190–91.

15 The parallels to Agamben's state of exception, in which the state is both included and excluded from its domain, are obviously strong here. See Giorgio Agamben, *Homo Sacer: Sovereign Power and Bare Life,* trans. Daniel Heller-Roazen (Stanford: Stanford University Press, 1998); *State of Exception,* trans. Kevin Attell (Chicago: University of Chicago Press, 2008).

16 The swerve is technically not a consequence of self-belonging, but rather of coincidence. That said, the swerve will be inexplicable to anyone who takes self-evident awareness as proof against colocated agents. Witness the impotent rage of the powerful.

at the bottom, where, no matter how precise the command or how willing the supplicant, some amount of swerve is always possible. The final arbiter can only give the *appearance* of causation, priming every startle with a master predicate until its magisterial will takes on the look and feel of a constant fact. Sensation (let it be fear potentiation) is made to do more work than it can handle, giving rise, as Althusser and others have pointed out, to a need to reproduce the stimulus over and over, in order to fend off the entropic event of the *collective* identity.

What radiance tells us is that we can't hope to practice object orientation in isolation from each other, because we're always already becoming entangled in each other's intentions. The encounter with being is to be sought, not at an authentic remove from the madding crowd, but precisely in the everydayness where our equality with other beings is most at risk. Yet once so entangled there, we end up having to choose between relativism and righteousness, subjectivity and sovereignty. So the question returns with a vengeance: How can we ever expect to reach an agreement about the exo-relations of our personal effects without invoking an absolute personal effect along the way?

The keen eye will note that science aims to satisfy this very desire: to present results that anyone can replicate, such that the *observer* is indifferent to identification. No doubt science has trouble when it comes to vague objects, which are broken for one person and merely mishandled for another, and it certainly stumbles, as I insisted earlier, on the question of what it's like to be a person. On other hand, it does a pretty good job at demonstrating that there *can be* observers indifferent to identification, and this finding is no small thing. For his part, Alexander has shown us that any person, regardless of what it's like to be a person, can refuse to respond at least in some part to some stimulus, and from there undertake a procedure that forces the grounds of another being into view. Grounds forcing puts each practitioner in the same ontological position, not of finding oneself, but of finding the outside, where the outside is not an object of scientific interest singled out in advance, but rather whatever the wilderness brings. Yet the procedure continues to be empirical with respect to the observer's access to this wilderness. It's not a metaphor or an analogy. It can be tested. It can be traced, lost, rediscovered — all of which is to say it can be *practiced,* as one practices the piano, for as long as one does.

In this respect, I think extended grounds forcing holds promise as an empirical venture, provided we can dispel the assumption that the observer exists only in the moment when a reproducible experiment is in progress. The most advantageous line of attack is, in fact, not on the isolated instance of a lab result, where replaceability comes cheap, but on the bridge operators that we build for ourselves in order to cross the many disconnected observations of our lives. Since these bridge operators are external to each of us, because what fills the gap is in the world, we pass from the presumption of circularity, in which I construct that which constructs me, to a less well-defined terrain, in which I am only one of many who "think into" that which constructs me. In the case of the absolute object, which is a simply a bridge operator openly admitted to be an artifact, I will have company when I abstain from altering it.

Extended grounds forcing will therefore call for an absolute object that intersects us severally, across our multitudinous flickerings of awareness. To meet the absolute personal effect head-on, it will also have to exist without any privileged claim as either token or type, an effect that reads nothing personal back to anyone, that prompts no intention and therefore simply exists, right where it is, in its unadorned factuality — an image of radiance *simpliciter.* My wager is that this set of conditions can be constructed and therefore tested, that the ability to force the grounds of our given intentions, those choices we do not choose, will be within our means if we can design an object to short-circuit reference at exactly those points where the absolute personal effect is reproduced — where unsubstantiated necessity, as we supposed in the beginning, is expressed as imminent.

Or rather, we can expect such a thing to test *us...*

In a sense, the idea behind extended grounds forcing is quite obvious: I can achieve mutual independence with a thing by avoiding physical contact with it. One could think of this abstention (which, wickedly, is the root meaning of the term *epoche*) as an imitation of withdrawal: I replay the inaccessibility of an object at the level of its local manifestation, so as to prove my lack of access to its virtual being. This independence can then be modulated to verify whether I can interact with the object in some way that doesn't fundamentally change its status as a type. The tricky part comes in stopping shy of the next step, which is, usually, to protect this absolute object from others and whatever ends they may have in store for it. To do that, after all, would be to make it an extension of my personal identity again, when its independence from me is the ongoing goal I originally set for myself.

Any absolute object worth its salt will therefore be something altogether common, in both senses of the word. It will have a halting point, in the sense that it will be within my power to approach it, to recognize it and, crucially, to reproduce it. At the same time, it will lack a halting point among our shared exo-relations, insofar as it serves as an extension of *any* declarative mind. Not being "for" anything or anyone in particular, there won't be any reason within the constraints of necessity to preserve it. Yet for all that, if it survives, it will have done so at the risk of destruction by parties other than just myself. And if it is destroyed, it can always be reintroduced without concern for narrative timing, since the stakes for reproducing it are low by design.

Extended grounds forcing does of course presuppose the *possibility* of shared interests by more than one party, to which I say: So be it. Possibility, in the larger sense, is exactly what we want to test. If nothing else, we know that an interest *in* shared interests is generally shared, because we see it so often when interests are at odds. The rarity is the straightforward commonality come to be.

My watchword going forward, then, will be to locate those shared obligatory practices that capture an object in mid-flight, and then to subtract every hint of an absolute personal effect from that object's composition. If what I'm advancing is correct, the result will be a set that's larger than our mutual obligations, because the object that results won't impose anything beyond the existence of obligation as such. And from there it will be but a short step, I hope, to a more general unraveling: the gradual emergence of entities from our deontic hold on them, as the iterative suspension of our ends gives way to a shared outside — a genuinely *public* domain that, despite the vast amounts of intellectual capital spent on it, we really know very little about: *A case of bone-handled toothbrushes, a mountain range on its first day of existence, three black ribbons in the grass...*

5

Public Things

The idea of a republic is anything but new to philosophy. Ever since Plato fleshed out his version of one, the concept has been visited with a regularity that would generally indicate a dead horse no longer worth treating in a politically incorrect manner. I have my own peculiar reason, however, to think there's breath in it yet. While the word "republic" suggests the double structure of "the people again," it actually derives from the Latin *res publica*, where *res* translates as "a substantive, concrete object." A republic, for the Roman, was not a concept at all, but a physical entity: a public *thing*.

In the following chapter, I'd like to take a tour of some objects that show potential as public things in this older, stranger sense. Some already exist in presentable form. Others can be projected or imagined by varying existing objects. In any event, the idea will be to force the grounds of an object for a class of humans (mathematical operators capable employing the axiom of replacement) — to render an object public, without falling prey to the snares of self-belonging. As before, when we scrutinized Alexander's thought experiment, a key move will be to restrict the replacement operation, but now the monotype will be extended to an object "out there," and therefore available to a class of coincident entities, any one of whom can force the object to exist on its own grounds by a refusal to incorporate it into any end. Such a result, if it occurs, I will call objective, and, because objectivity entails that an object occupy its own place in relation to humans, I will go on the original meaning of the word *ethos* as "habitat" and regard the result as ethical. In my book, objectivity *is* ethical.[1]

This exercise will plainly be fragile at all times, since anyone can alter the composition of any object at will, simply by declaring some member of the class as its foundational nexus. The exo-relations of a public thing will have a hard time surviving the comment section of an online news story. The exercise won't be absolutely fragile, either, though, because objects as they exist independently of us aren't instantly perishable anymore than they are inherently permanent. We know that they present degrees of resistance to their destruction, even if we can't predict the degree in advance. They have *some* degree of negentropy. In this sense, the carpentry I have in mind will expand the potential for grounds forcing by enlisting matter to do a share of the work that others might reserve for human thinkers only. A public thing is like Otto's notebook, with the twist that we count on an object to think *itself* for us. But it should also be said that the externalist view I've adopted does not let *us* off the hook. It only claims parity between internal and external operators — and parity is in fact an excellent synonym for equal footing among beings. Our share of the work, should we choose to accept it, will be to methodically suspend the linking of one thing to another — to practice thinking the independent identity over time of an effect we've lodged somewhere in the world.

This tension between outer and inner, between the behavior of matter and our ability to weave that behavior into an iterative procedure, will determine the efficacy of each public thing. Before we didn't have to worry about this tension so much, because the object was the body, which is always there (making the body, in a sense, the gateway to the extended mind). A public thing, on the other hand, is external by its nature, so we will have to admit to uneven access to it, and then see what can be done to "bring it to zero" and so initiate a diagonalization.

---

[1] As I hope I have made clear, an objective ethics will be also be a virtue ethics, in the sense that it maintains a practice without predicting specific ethical problems.

For much the same reasons, the examples I've found don't obey readymade exposition. I can only draw from my own corner of the universe, with its indigenous attractions. As a matter of choice (based inevitably on convenience, as choices will be), my plan is to start from a consensus between two parties—a pact—building up to larger classes, and from there to classes of classes. This choice appears to project a path of increasing technological complexity, passing through the principles of possession, dispossession and circulation, and finally to a slant departure from them all. But for all the appearance of a cumulative strategy, each of these thought experiments is conceived as being independent of the primary decontrol, and, by the same count, independent of each other. There is no progression to mastery, nor is there any downside that I can see to pursuing them in combination.

The Shape of Agreements To Come

Throughout much of Western history, when two parties wanted to enter into a contract with each other, they undertook a procedure called indenture. The principle was quite simple. The agreement was written twice on the same piece of parchment, the parchment cut in two in a somewhat haphazard fashion, and one half given to each party. The resulting cut created unique tooth-like shapes (the Latin for "tooth" being *dent-*, therefore "indenture") that formed a perfect match between copies. In this way, an agreement could be confirmed at a later date simply by putting the documents together. Sometimes, the terms were written out in triplicate, with a third copy given to a neutral party, just in case someone lost a copy, or cheated.

Indenture was often an article of servitude, drawn up when some poor soul was unable to pay a debt. Even today, well into the age of paperless contracts, the term "indentured servant" carries some of its original sting. But now imagine a document of indenture, torn in two as per the custom, with one minor, seemingly trivial change: Nothing is written on it. Not having any terms, such a document would have an entirely different status from the traditional one. In fact, its terms would be precisely those under which its validity was tested and the *terms* of that validity found to fail.[2]

As it turns out, blank indenture is pretty good suggesting an intention without providing one. We can see intuitively that the match between the two halves establishes something true about matter: The match indicates agreement. We can see, too, that this agreement is made not by declaration, but by a procedure, for which, oddly, we can give no account. The contract is just itself, in the world, independent of its parties. It also allows for a fairly wide field of types of contractual partners. When investigating the behavior of mirror neurons in macaque monkeys, scientists have discovered a significantly high firing rate in response to... ripping a sheet of paper in half.[3] We might feel emboldened, then, to believe that the range of a public thing might be expanded to include other species. (Going forward, I'll just let that possibility hang.)

The blank indenture also exhibits the subtle connection between foundation and choice we identified as a hallmark of the implicit mind: It ranges over the domain of potential agreements and disagreements without necessitating any of them. If you were to assert the necessity of the object, you would have to do so on some grounds not given by the object. You could never hold up your half and air any grievances safeguarded by the contract, because the contract safeguards nothing. The object forces the thought of agreement to a position of contingency.

Things start to get iffy, however, if we try to identify a blank indenture's exo-relations. The persuasiveness of its physical

---

[2] One can find a precedent for the blank indenture in the Greek *symbolon*, which captured the same principle of physically agreeing parts in a broken clay object. I chose to consider the indenture as a potential public thing instead of the symbolon because, despite the great temptation to follow the etymology to the word "symbol," pieces of paper are more readily available than clay pots.

[3] Evelyne Kohler et al., "Hearing Sounds, Understanding Actions: Action Representation in Mirror Neurons," *Science* 297 (August 2, 2002): 846–48.

match seems to apply only to itself, with no obvious relation to *any* terms. To illustrate the point, we can cast it as a Latour litany:

Street lamps, medieval armor, calendar, blank indenture

The mere inclusion of the indenture on this list does little to challenge the necessity of any particular relation to the objects. On the contrary, some of the objects appear as types without tokens. It would be a little odd, for example, to argue about street lamps as a concept. In short, we find ourselves without a formal context on which our unnecessary object might operate. This, it should be said, is a characteristic of Latour litanies in general. By their nature, they present declarative rather than procedural terms, leaving the reader with nothing to diagonalize.

We might expect to improve the situation, then, by shifting our attention to the carpentry of a specific case in which two parties have a relation to the token instances of objects. Since I entered into just such a contract with a co-worker once, I'll show the new list accordingly:

Street lamps, medieval armor, calendar, blank indenture entered into by Jeff and Dave

Now we begin to have a structure with some bite to it. Both Jeff and I might have an opinion about medieval armor, but it's not likely to be a strong one. The same cannot be said for our relation to the calendar, because, at the time we entered into this experimental contract, we worked together, I as the author of the instructions on the calendar, he as one who carried them out. One jot of my magic marker could impose an undue burden on him, or make his day pleasant and productive. So our litany is no longer hypothetical. We've moved from the assertion of a flat ontology to the realm of practice, where some objects are closer than others.

It seems fair to say that our blank indenture acted as a kind of external conscience for Jeff and I during the time we worked together. Our complementary objects gave us a precedent to refuse to disagree (or to go ahead and disagree) as equals, whenever either of us arrived at a crossroads between consensus and discord. Part and parcel to this freedom was a predisposition to break down the steps involved in a task — to forego the descriptive label of some given goal in favor of a closer discussion of the smaller increments involved. Our orientation shifted from "knowing that" to "knowing how."

Still, the blank indenture turns out to be useful mostly as counterfactual example of a monotype, because it never quite gives us the rigor of grounds forcing we would like. First and foremost, it seems to lack opportunities for iteration. At what point, after all, do these whimsical scraps actually enter into the rest of our activities? With the Alexandrian directions, the command "head up and forward" can always be invoked, because — quite simply — wherever you go, there you are. The blank indenture, on the other hand, seems to "happen" only once, and nothing in it indicates any rule for reuniting its parts or avoiding their reunion, for preserving them or abandoning them to the elements, or any other action on them. It doesn't make any sense to believe that our matching pieces of paper will just magically appear before our eyes whenever we want to force the grounds of our relationship onto the wider context around us. Our options, in fact, are either to remember them *in absentia,* at the sacrifice of any procedural engagement, or to keep them physically at hand — say, in our respective personal spaces — which limits the procedural engagement to the two of us.

By the nature of the *object,* a blank indenture encourages a procedure based on possession. This is easy to see if we imagine tearing the paper into smaller bits to include more participants, a strategy sure to become daunting as the puzzle pieces approach the size of postage stamps, to say nothing of the quandaries posed by non-neighboring pieces that form no match at all. It just doesn't work very well except for pairs of participants.

That said, it does frame the capacity for objectivity at the limited level of a partnership. Identical wedding rings, sufficiently designed to lack referents, could, for example, objectify an ethics for their bearers. Whatever pre-conceived notions two partners may bring to a marriage, the objects on their fingers, which really do exist, act as a termless agreement that systematically outstrips each of those notions in turn. No one knows the limit of the contract. No doubt it could be argued that wedding rings aren't crucial for a relationship to function. If one of the partners misplaced hers, it wouldn't necessarily signal the dissolution of the pact. But that's exactly the point. The partners wear them *even though* they're not necessary.

Deflating as it may seem, objects as familiar as these can lay bare the reality of things — and almost certainly are doing so right now, in unsung locations the world over. *This* kind of event is underway often, using plainly traditional carpentry, without the windfall of a rare opening onto the void.

Of course, the implication here is that "identical objects as pacts" will be subject to the same constraints of limited possession as indenture is. But are they? Let's look at the pluses and minuses using another example. Not long ago, my elder son took a fierce interest in a certain kind of bracelet-weaving that some of his friends were learning. I don't know how many children across the globe were immersing themselves in this activity, but the loom was commercially available on the cheap, so one would imagine the numbers were fairly high. There seemed to be no romantic angle to making them, and no fictional character inciting further purchases. It was just a fad that bubbled up and passed, with no particular goal attached. Given the parameters I've set out, such fads, in which no end is evident, satisfy at least the basics of grounds forcing. What's missing, on one hand, is some explicit built-in structure to prevent the assignment of a function linking personal identity to possession — to cliques within the fad population — and on the other, some matrix of obligation to hold the activity in place.

Leaving Out the Most Important Part

Well then, if possessing objects gives rise to issues of personal-identity assignment, what about the opposite? Suspending for a moment the emotional overtones associated with the word, and thinking more specifically about spatial relations, we could train our sights on a procedure that *excludes* an object from a class and leaves the inclusion of humans in that class as a free variable. After all, we originally identified the chain of intention as beginning with an absolute object that we choose not to touch, even though we can. Abstention could, in principle, help to solve the problem of self-belonging by turning custody into a negative. Instead of "everyone here has x equally," we would get "none of us here has x."

We don't have to invent such cases from scratch. If you went looking for large, decentralized classes of humans, it wouldn't take long before you came across a familiar organization that also began as a pact between two parties, and has since grown to provide a remarkably developed version of a public thing, based on just this kind of inversion.

While Alcoholics Anonymous has often been branded as an evil cult, my exposure to it suggests something closer to the description given by one of its founders — a "benign anarchy."[4] According to the canonical version of its genesis, Bill Wilson was unable to achieve lasting sobriety until he met Dr. Bob Smith and they agreed to help each other to banish alcohol from their lives. This agreement, made between self-declared equals, looks at first glance like an ordinary pact, but in fact it both excluded an object and decentered foundation in a single stroke. How to maintain the exclusion while maintaining its lack of a center then became the basis for everything that followed.

Among their first strategies was to radicalize their idea of time. Like the body, addiction is always present, and for the alcoholic, the stimulus to drink is always imminent. But then, so is the ability to refuse to respond to this stimulus. Bill W. and Dr. Bob, as they came to call themselves, realized that, although they couldn't control their addiction through a declared goal,

---

4   As one might guess, my personal communications on the subject are anonymous, but see *Alcoholics Anonymous: The Story of How Many Thousands of Men and Women Have Recovered from Alcoholism* (New York: Alcoholics Anonymous World Services, Inc., 2001).

they could always tell themselves, "I do not have to drink the *next* drink." They could refuse to respond to the stimulus, and track their sobriety *at the moment they were speaking*. As this strategy started to work, the declaration took on the form of a partially ordered set, much like Alexander's "all at once, one after the other," but here expressed in a longer sequence: {now} ≤ {now, today} ≤ {now, today, total number of days of accumulated sobriety}.

Insofar as the AA member can insert this monotype ("I do not have to drink the next drink") into any sequence of events, we can clearly recognize the procedure of grounds forcing. As the alcoholic reiterates it and stays sober "one day at a time," while also counting the cumulative days of continuous sobriety, her daily actions are forced to unfold in a way that she can longer choose in advance. The procedure renders the objective independence of the alcoholic and the alcohol *from each other* on an iterative, ongoing basis. As before, the ethics amounts to a virtue ethics, in that good results are presumed to come from the initial affirmation of a value, here the affirmation of the separation from a contingent thing. The set of actions can be brought to zero, and so can be diagonalized, and the diagonalized act, whatever it may be, can always be paired with the explicit action of "not drinking."

These aspects of AA obtain at the level of an individual. Where the tradition begins to function more clearly as a public thing is in the use of space. AA members don't presume the *solution* to imminent need to be always at hand, but instead go *to* a location—the so-called rooms—to attend meetings. In this way, they solve the problem that arises if a public thing is a moveable object. We're no longer talking about an object that belongs to coincident entities. It's the coincident entities, the humans, who are contained in the object. Yet for all that, membership in the space is not guarded or regulated in any way. There are no written lists of attendance or registration records, and there are no membership consequences for "going out to do more research," as returning to drink is called. One simply starts "counting days" again — or doesn't.[5]

Granted, some of the tenets of AA may seem to violate our prohibition on self-belonging, such as its emphasis on a religious experience and the associated affirmation of a deity. On closer inspection, however, the presumption of a set of all sets dissolves. This dissolution follows directly from the rule of unrestricted membership. Although the organization began by invoking a Christian god, practical experience caused its founding element to be recast as "a higher power as we understood it," because, so the lore has it, the relation of membership only functioned when it was member-defined. As a result, even if some members define the group as theistic, the "contract," such as it is, still allows for an inner model of the group to be constructed without resorting to such a predicate. One does not have to declare allegiance to anything or anyone, or even to attend meetings for that matter; desire alone is sufficient. While it might seem clever to point out that a high*er* power is not necessarily the high*est* power, that is, in fact, how the set theory of AA plays out. As a result, the tradition defies the kind of declarative totalization often associated with monotheism.

Leaving Out Many of the Most Important Parts

A great deal of AA's clarity derives from the absence of degrees in its excluded object. One either absorbs alcohol into the bloodstream or does not. There is no middle ground. This appearance of the law of the excluded middle and the ongoing inability to secure it through willpower is what definitively establishes the axiom of choice outside the declarative mind and reorganizes the needs of a sober life into an iterative set. Obviously, most

---

[5] The physical separation from an object, accomplished through the formation of a group in which each individual "I"-intention seeks to further that separation, might provide new material for the study of "we"-intentions. For investigations along this line, see Michael Wilby, "Subject, Mode and Content in We-intentions," in *Phenomenology and Mind* (2012), http://philpapers.org/archive/WILSMA-4.pdf (accessed Feburary 24, 2015).

people can't be so definitively cornered. Even organizations patterned after AA don't generally enjoy the same level of stringency. Members of Overeaters Anonymous, for example, still have to eat, and their ability to force independence from at least one class of objects is attenuated accordingly. So we might wonder if grounds forcing that excludes a particular object from a class is a specialized case.

It's certainly thought-provoking in this regard that among the very earliest characteristics of human behavior was a prohibition on eating, or sometimes even touching, one specific kind of animal or plant. Once again we return to the notion of an absolute object initiating the chain of intention. The totemic taboo, as this ban has been retroactively called, prevailed across the spectrum of non-agricultural cultures and, in addition to the ban on contact, often involved a declared kinship with the totemic entity. A century ago, a fair amount of ink was spilled explaining totemism and taboos, until the subject proved intractable and the scholarly community moved on. Yet our accrued findings might shed new light on the practice, especially if we regard it not as a fixed structure, as the tendency has been, but simply as an available strategy for resolving the anxiety of radiance. For the totemist as much as the alcoholic, after all, the observance of the taboo stabilizes a baseline fact: If I belong to the fox clan, then my body does not come in contact with a fox.

Such a parallel might seem superficial, but since we're concerned with carpentry rather than immutable structures, we can afford to be curious. We can afford, for example, to think about the stakes. We can see that the alcoholic is bent on self-destruction, and that the turn to recovery techniques is based on survival, even if personal will is renounced. But what drives the totemist to follow this same counterintuitive rule?

A clue may come from what we've learned from the axiom schema of replacement. For all the attention paid to the basis and motivation for identifying with a totemic being, one interesting fact has been overlooked: The totem is invariably not a specific being, but a *type* of being. The prohibition is not against eating *that* fox, but against eating foxes *per se*.[6] I submit on this basis — brashly maybe, but there it is — that the totemic taboo reveals the dim appearance of indifference to identification in the human object, and the remote onset of our coincident entities. Such a hypothesis might help to explain why totemism seems to have appeared without a decent explanation from its practitioners. When interviewed by sociologists in the heyday of structuralism, totemic subjects generally had no good answer as to when the behavioral pattern began. It was just "always that way." For our part we may add: It was always that way because the reporter — the latecomer coincident entity — came to be along with the report. On the flip side, one can better understand the belief, pervasive throughout totemic cultures, that a violation of the taboo resulted in instant death. So long as the fox and the fox-human remained materially separate, an intentional relation to the world was vouchsafed. That's what was at stake: the entropic event of the account, at a time when there was very little account at all. Eat the totem and you — the declarative you — go to pieces.

Note, too, that the taboo was apparently not always enough on its own to prevent disaster. The other taboo that frequently appeared alongside the ban on touching the totem was the prohibition on incest. In light of our inquiry, we can advance that this bias toward exogamy — marrying outside one's own totem — was an additional "found" strategy for decentering the declarative mind. Rather than being strictly instinctively based, it was a way of preventing the *name* of the totem from totalizing the human type. By definition, the totemic entities notionally

---

[6] Freud mentions the assignment of the totem to a type, by way of quoting J.G. Frazer: "[a]s distinguished from a fetich [sic], a totem is never an isolated individual but a class of objects, generally a species of animals or of plants, more rarely a class of inanimate natural objects, very rarely a class of artificial objects." Sigmund Freud, *Totem and Taboo: Resemblances Between the Psychic Lives of Savages and Neurotics* (New York: Vintage, 1946), 134. While it's pleasing to see such a tidy list, the connection between mathematical classes and objects has not, to my knowledge, previously been made in the literature on totemism.

paired in a conjugal union — say, fox and sparrow — could have no biological result, and therefore could not be unified according to their own terms. While the totem-exogamy structure clearly did not allow for the unrestricted inclusion of members, since it followed a strict rule of progeny, it did provide a means of accounting for "everyone" without closing the system. The substitution formula *par excellence* — the name — could not be used to describe a set of all sets. There was no species called "man."

While the causes driving the demise of totemism are beyond the scope of this inquiry, the fragility of its membership structure is easy to see. My admittedly armchair theory is that domestication — which from a totemist perspective involved nothing less than "adults breastfeeding from the relatives" — was a violent game changer. The conquest of other beings was just too much of a shock. *And still is.* There is a way in which the appropriation of all things and the correlation of all things are linked, in which an object "for us" comes to be treated as existing for us.

In this respect, we can assume that now, as then, any practice can always be overrun by a stronger system. When the state *orders* someone to attend AA meetings, for example, as sometimes happens, its principle of unrestricted membership summarily collapses.

It's at this point that the pessimists appear to have the stronger argument: All roads lead to Rome. Then again, if that's where they lead, maybe the thing to do is go there. If excluding an object limits the range of participants as much as sharing one does, we might consider an object that can be either possessed *or* surrendered — and that currently enjoys the status of *the* expression of imminent necessity.

What To Do with Those Pennies

It's a striking fact that, in an age when money is said to define all things, it circulates almost not at all. More and more, financial exchanges take place digitally, beyond the engagement of the implicit mind, while the bank note and the coin are treated like relics of the past. Of course, there's no reason to believe that yesterday's way should have lasted forever. Bank notes themselves are a fairly recent invention, and coins, though older, did not come to us fresh from the Big Bang. Nonetheless, an object that passes from hand to hand throughout a wide population is practically tailor-made for a study in objective ethics. The next stop on our speculative tour, then, will not involve an appeal to nostalgia so much as a glimpse into a function that a circulating object may yet come to have: an inner model of cash.

On one level, bills and coins are specific tokens, each to themselves. One can know that this exact thing, with its unique serial number, has been handled by others before, and will be again. The brute materiality of cash has instilled the understandable belief that it is not entirely sanitary.[7] On the other hand, it has also served to join large reaches of matter into a sprawling weblike colocation, long before the handiwork of spiders became a popular metaphor. This *extended* colocation, as it were, has historically involved a clear demarcation of the possession and dispossession of an object external to oneself. One accepts cash physically and surrenders it just as physically, and so the object circulates… physically.

Oddly, one can also isolate a level at which cash lacks reference. One need not be literate to recognize a dollar bill. Its identity is constituted by a precise design and the material on which that design is fixed. This precision of design elements allows cash to be falsified: There is something that it is and something that it's not. It's not only strongly a token, but also strongly a type.

So cash ought to be the best bridge operator one can imagine. It has a form that by general decree can't be altered, it travels

---

[7] Recent studies have focused on the pathogens present on dollar bills. What such studies fail to address is the rise of autoimmune disorders and antibiotic-resistant diseases during the same time period in which the circulation of paper money has dwindled. See Michaeleen Doucleff, "Dirty Money: A Microbial Jungle Thrives in Your Wallet," *Shots: Health News* from NPR (April 23, 2014), http://www.npr.org/sections/health-shots/2014/04/23/305890574/dirty-money-a-microbial-jungle-thrives-in-your-wallet (accessed August 25, 2016).

everywhere, and there's wide consensus as to its validity. One could go so far as to say that currency secures a relation between objects and rational numbers at the level of our ongoing intentions. There's just one bothersome detail. Out of its design, which would be a mere shape or bald presentation if we were somehow deprived of our personal identity, there appears a building, a star, a face. The object is a representation for something else.

And here comes that problem again. In a domain of objects defined by object x, object x is supposed to define all of the objects in the domain, yet at the very least some physical act must be employed to produce x as distinct from $\sim x$, that x is $\sim\sim x$, and moreover, to verify that it continues to be $\sim\sim x$ between time 1 and time 2. Some entity must therefore define the defining entity — in this case, a human somewhere to guard against counterfeit. The OOO case for humans as objects is particularly strong here. It makes *more* sense to categorize the human as an object than not to do so, because categorizing the human as an object exposes monetization for what it is — a case of Russell's paradox.

Any entity that defines a defining object must hold a contradictory place in an account where common sense is to prevail. There is no getting out of it. Currency is an absolute personal effect, which can never completely stabilize the very numerical array it exists to put right. Thus one sees extravagant allegories of the issuer's origin, generally referencing some moment when no law was in effect (war, divinity, etc.), as the grounds for its authority. Thus too, displays of its authority in which, in some cases, the absolute personal effect can be falsified only on pain of death.

That's pretty rich stuff. Let's unpack it a little.

When I assert that currency secures a relation between objects and rational numbers, I don't mean that currency determines a numerical value through some sort of animistic miracle. I mean simply that currency allows for a rational number to be assigned to matter in a relation of belonging, insofar as it functions as an external bridge operator. In fact, we can also see a connection here to our time-honored standby, the axiom of choice. As will be recalled, the axiom of choice says that for any collection of non-empty bins, one can choose at least one element from each bin. In a situation where currency circulates, one can, likewise, choose a number corresponding to any object presented without knowing in advance how many instances of this object there are. You don't need to know how many apples exist in the world before setting a price for your own. Your number may be too high to move them, or too low to make a profit, but you can come up with one, because, as has oft been said, everything has its price. If you haggle with a customer, you won't end up at a price with an endless remainder, even if you extend a credit line. No one is ever going to have to pay you π.

So the issuer, by minting a currency, is guaranteeing the soundness of arithmetic for the material world in the next, so-far-unlived moment. The soundness of arithmetic certainly seems like a good thing, and one can see why advocates of the free market tacitly or openly appeal to the clarity of the rational numbers. In the elegant sheen of digits, everything seems to make sense. But if what I'm saying is true, the guarantee of rational numbers introduces irrationality elsewhere within the system. Anyone can in effect owe the *issuer* an endless decimal like π, because the issuer, as authenticator of the currency, belongs to the range of circulation while behaving as if it doesn't, and so can decide as it likes when a debt is paid.

History has seen various methods of resolving this fundamental problem, none of them, in my view, successful. We've already noted the reference to supernatural origins. The attempt to commodify the universe seems to reach a limit when it comes to inaccessible objects like stars, allowing issuers at least to dodge the problem of self-belonging. But then, it's hard to maintain one's descent from Alpha Centauri. This may be why currencies sometimes reference an abstract principle in language instead — say, a transcendent deity, or Progress. Of course, these abstractions will have a different meaning for the issuer and its people, because they simply have no objectivity in the sense I have defined the term. They exist differently in different humans.[8]

The opposite problem arises if the issuer evokes ties to the land, by placing an image of, say, a native tree or landscape on a bank note. The bounded space of a nation solves the relation of belonging, in that its members can be reduced to a nominally finite head count in a finite space, but it still gives the issuer no means of resolving the self-belonging actor — unless an outsider should materialize, ready to invade that space. The outsider seems to solve the problem, because it relieves the issuer of the burden of asserting the totality of sets. Under the threat of a common enemy, which actually has to be contextualized as the native tree or landscape under threat, one can find a sense of purpose. But at this point, the "someone else" accorded the grounds for the axiom of choice also threatens one's physical existence. The rest is theater: Anyone who takes on the job of authentication will be beholden to enforce the sanctity of $2+2=4$ on an illogical basis.

While a world currency might look tempting as a way out of this problem, it too would only function through the arbitrary creation of a nonsensical exterior. It's certainly ironic that Bertrand Russell, whose paradox changed the course of mathematics, should have advocated world government in his later years.[9] In such a case — assuming the global power issued its own currency — the axiom of choice would still need to be borrowed from somewhere, and the declared integrity of its decision defended. Mathematics and violence would still be weirdly linked.

---

8   Abstract slogans seem to be what Laclau has in mind for his empty signifier, which comes to signify ever longer chains of equivalence until, as he says: "at the limit it will be pure communitarian being independent of all concrete manifestation." Ernesto Laclau, *Emancipation(s)* (London: Verso, 2007), 42. Yet he doesn't seem to take into account the possibility that different parties can imbue the empty signifier with contradictory meanings that are only discovered later, when some connection to a concrete manifestation is attempted. And you thought the stuff in the refrigerator was all shared.

9   Bertrand Russell, *The Impact of Science on Society* (New York: Simon and Schuster, 1953).

Our options are still not entirely exhausted. If reducing the number of authenticators does nothing to resolve the paradox, what about reducing the appearance of the defining object — not abolishing money outright, communist-style, but settling for the demise of cash? It might seem that structuring money as a vast unit of account, as is presently the case with digital currencies, has already put an end to any pretense of an absolute personal effect. Yet our ethical reading of the situation allows us to see that this is not the case at all. The numbers on computer screens in two locations may amount to the same topological shapes, but the personal effects that the expressed numbers occupy never actually coincide. Meanwhile, the consequences of the contradiction continue unabated. Though the building, the star, the face do not necessarily appear anywhere in the transaction, their function has been condensed into the symbol for the currency, and remain as active there as ever. Anyone who doubts this need only consider a world where $1 = 1.28$. That's a possible outcome if one removes the symbols for the currencies, say the dollar sign and euro mark, from a published exchange rate. The authenticator who seems to have vanished is only concealed — and likely to be a little rusty in its aim when it resurfaces to quell the latest challenge to its authority.

In this respect, crypto-currencies, even though they're independent of government authority, suffer from the same ethical shortcomings as any digital currency, insofar as they're units of account subject to an exchange rate. Aside from any virtues it may hold as a monetary unit, Bitcoin, for example, was expressly designed to eliminate the need for trust. Yet the trader in Bitcoins, who presumably has a stake in the success of the currency, still has to trust that the architects of the system are playing fair.

For all their dizzying diversity, the various efforts to block Russell's paradox share one assumption: that a solution is necessary. To which one says, "of course." The mad king must be stopped, democracy must come, a change must come. Then again, it doesn't follow that a stated imperative brings about change. On the contrary, I've presented at least two existing cases where the unnecessary brings about the unforeseen, and where the good, though it can't be willed, occurs nonetheless. More to the point, the entire enterprise of arrogating relations between objects runs counter to our original interest in decentering the human in practice. It should be acknowledged in this respect that the ordinary bearer of a coin relies on the issuer to take on the burden of the paradox for the sake of everyday convenience. ("When working out a sequence of choice functions on rational numbers, it may help to think of them as being generated by someone else.") Logically then, we might want to shift our attention to the class of issuers — the many sovereign powers who, as self-described arbiters, are beholden in the last instance to no agreement with each other — and see what it would take to force the grounds of the absolute object outside of *them*.

First, let's recapitulate. In considering Alexander's directions, we found that, by forcing the grounds of a proposed action, we were able to establish a foundation for the actions of another entity (our strange companion) without expressly placing that foundation under our will. To move the head up and forward is an action that lies outside our ability either to do or not to do, because the command "head up and forward" *a)* does not submit to free volition and *b)* does occur to notable benefit under other conditions. As already remarked, it's known that among mammals the head typically leads the action in the same way that it does among humans when the directions are successful. Thus, the directions identify an outcome that can be verified as a disjunct from the power to name. In fact, they align with the most widely accepted means of blocking the paradox of self-belonging: downward inheritance.

In ZFC set theory, sets belonging to themselves are prevented by the axiom of foundation, which states that for every set there is a disjunct element — a set that is "lower down" in a sequence. Because every non-empty set is larger than the empty set, a non-empty set can usually be saved from self-belonging by being founded on the empty set. In the case of human thought, foundation is more difficult to achieve, because even the thought of the empty set belongs to thought. That's the crux of correlationism. For grounds forcing, the idea is to follow the downward inheritance of a predicated set until predication is surpassed, yet emptiness is still not attained. The Alexandrian directions reduce the possibility of predicated actions to zero, and still the body moves. A blank indenture, for its part, is neither empty nor predicated — its matching contours already agree, independent of the word "agree." This indirect choice of a number between 0 and 1, between nothing and a predicate, is evidence of an entity outside the declarative mind.

In the case of currency, then, we could envision a simple visual addition to cash that refers to no personal identity at all, and is therefore literally outside thought. Simply mint a banknote or coin according to its generally established design (just as we took actions as they were proposed), including all of its permanent references to sovereignty, and then *add* a mark — on the reverse, where commemorative images are usually found — that has no relation to any specific issuer. To really do it right, go further and choose a mark that can't even be construed as having a relation to any specific issuer, past, present, or future. This mark, lacking verifiable reference or provenance, would be fatherless, an orphan in the land of obligations.[10]

Assuming an initial satisfaction of these stipulations, we could also begin to imagine a codified structure: Inscribe the mark on the reverse or "tails" side, as mentioned — but only on the *lowest* denomination of the currency. Placement at the bottom, where the common prevails, would serve both to acknowledge the least work necessary to produce it, and to highlight the least element in the set, which, technically, is included in any higher figure named.

What would we achieve by this? Could a blank reference on the tail side of a penny or the back of a yuan ever be anything more than decoration — a curiosity in the history of commemorative coins? Several aspects, I believe, would help to raise such a mark above triviality. As an effect produced by a state, its absence of reference could be defined strictly, as a matter of

---

10 Those interested in an example are invited to turn to the appendix.

law. The domain of necessity would consequently be quite clear, leaving no question as to whether it "really happened" or not. It would also be contained *within* a precisely defined physical object and therefore would be present whenever the legitimacy of the object came under scrutiny — that is, at the point where the finality of the arbiter is reproduced. Unlike a blank indenture, which is procedurally vague, it would follow an established pattern of inclusion and exclusion for the participants as it passed from hand to hand. These instances would then become a partially ordered set, in which successive parties to a transaction were presented with a command to recognize the numericity of objects as defined by the state (the object's status as legal tender) and, simultaneously, a command that comes from nowhere and, by law, commands nothing.

A command from the state that commands nothing sounds fairly shocking, until you realize that it amounts to an acknowledgment of the general will, some paraphrase of which appears in the pages of many democratic constitutions. Our main interest here, however, lies not in political theory per se but in the connection that's revealed between the general will and the wider practice of object orientation. A strictly anonymous emblem would, by its very dead-endedness, prompt the bearer of the coin on which it's placed to evaluate it without recourse to any grounds for the axiom of choice — without halting at the issuer as its reason for being — thus opening an aperture in the declarative mind onto the objecthood of money. Pretty good for a lowly decoration!

And maybe too good. The peculiar, nameless, subjectless object that I'm proposing exudes an all-or-nothing quality, seeming at one moment to be a frivolous indulgence, at the next a recipe for insurrection. Drawing from our previous examples, we can see that this wavering quality stems from its potential for totalization. As laid out, my plan fails to explicitly rule out a set of all sets, because the entire effect exists at the pleasure of the issuer, thereby allowing the mark to be "the mark of issuer x" — which is very much like "my thought of the empty set" or, say, Dave Lindsay's Account of Nothing. The issuer, for whom knowledge of the mark is most direct, has no clear way of knowing when its own custody turns to jealousy, and the bearer has no particular reason not to be cynical about that ambiguity.

Fortunately, a mark chosen for its downward inheritance from *all* currency offers a provisional escape hatch out of this fix. Because my lowly decoration exists without any punitive consequences for its counterfeit, *other* issuers can adopt it without fear of infringement. In fact, any issuer whatsoever could reproduce it on its own legally binding design. A kind of copylefted seal, it could appear on different currencies, including alternative currencies, powerful currencies, weak currencies and currencies yet to be.

This radically public characteristic sets up an interesting dynamic. I've asserted that the concept of sovereignty supposes an inner sanctum with no relation to other issuers — in the case of monetization, this is the same as saying that the exchange rate between them is ungoverned.[11] Treasuries are fundamentally other to each other, because each one claims to be the founding element of the set of all sets. We saw in totemism a tendency toward exogamy that prevented this claim of totalization. The offspring of two different clans did not produce a new species, but rather multiplied relations between species, as fox-sparrows aligned with bear-coyotes, and so on in widening spirals with varying traditions of eventual collapse and reset. The issuer of currency, on the other hand, has nowhere to go but to reproduce its exact expression of agency.

Adoption across currencies thus becomes the saving grace, because it breaks the presumption of totality. A mark of "no authority" placed on the effects of inviolable authority (bills or coins with an expressed denomination) would then act as a pressure on the smallest subset for cash *as cash*. The structure of grounds forcing now comes into view on a second level: If these different least elements were brought together in a strictly

---

11 Continuing the comparison to Harman's ontology: An exchange rate as a passive outcome of sovereign monetary policies suggests a lack of available vicars to bring issuers of currency into causal relation with each other.

procedural sense, the irresolvable relation between the various "smallest" rational numbers (penny, yuan, dinar, ..., n) would theoretically force some even smaller founding element, which cannot be named and yet represents some value greater than zero. The result: The participating *issuers* would no longer be foundational in their own eyes, but subsets of a larger, unnamable set.[12]

How naive is it to imagine that an organization such as, say, the International Anti-Counterfeiting Coalition would bring together coins from different nations, each bearing a "trans-sovereign" mark, there to be exposed in all their unprotected ontic glory? How audacious is it to think that cash will be even be minted in years to come? I have no idea. One cannot insist on the absence of authority, of course, and in this sense an open-ended adoption or evaluation cannot be controlled. It's not necessary that it's necessary. Moreover, cash lacks the advantage of the blank indenture, which, by the very act of ripping it in half, implicates two parties directly in some collaboration from the get-go.

On the other hand, the logic underpinning the proposal is at least consistent with our original assumption that the correlation has to be defeated from within (with the issuer taking over the post, sometimes occupied by the Cartesian ego, of the master predicate that ranges over a class), and if no one takes it up, one can nonetheless get a sense from it of the distance between present conditions and an objective ethics. Conversely, if it were attempted and ascribed to some ulterior agency — a plot to form a world government or the feeble attempts of a few misguided dreamers — the failure would merely signal a return to the way things already are.

We also have reason to believe that it would be good if such a mark were adopted on the penny and the yuan and the dinar, and indeed on any x currency whatsoever, including alternative currencies, since, as a mark that *anyone* can guarantee, it would introduce an element that exceeds any one authority. There

---

12 It bears recalling that Aristotle tutored the young Alexander the Great, who lived to put his own image on a coin.

would be no master predicate to found the forced set. The test therefore would be to maintain its rightful use by the *next* participant, whoever they might be, without regard to their status as friend or foe. If OOO entails that you *show* some object to be independent of your mind, then its efficacy in at least one instance would constitute a minimal demonstration, at the level of pure procedure, of identification with your enemy. That would be the practice elicited by the mark — the way of being of the objective ethics so posed.

In speculating on candidates for public things, currency offers a well-established and highly codified system with a very wide range of use. It also has a triumphant ring to it, in that it proceeds up to what appears to be the limit case of possible classes and then decenters *that*. As far as I can tell, it's an open question as to whether there are any further levels of classes susceptible to grounds forcing — classes of classes of classes. The answer to that would seem to rely on the identification of some external monotype for a class larger than humans, which the present inquiry is unable to provide (except maybe somewhere in that teaser about macaque monkeys).

Then again, it may be that economic sovereignty will yet be exceeded as a domain of imminent necessity. After all, if totemism went the way of all things, so too could the central banks. In this respect, we can entertain variations on public things that show some potential, not only to surpass sovereignty, but also to yield more immediate development — and more egalitarian access.

Sounding the Wilderness

The early phase of the Occupy movement was notable for its absence of leadership or clear goals. Though its appearance can be traced through certain motivating parties, no one spoke for it, and it sought audience with no one in particular. It's easy to see the parallel between this purposelessness and the general outlines of grounds forcing. To a street identified with the imminent necessity of the capitalism, the monotype command "occupy" is applied. A human without portfolio, with no particular qualities of note, assents to this command, goes to a plaza on that street and, if she so desires, addresses the other humans there. The content of her speech is neither accepted nor rejected out of hand: The others present actually refuse to respond to it, and instead *develop a procedure* for relaying the speech in radiating waves, in a formalized method called the human microphone, such that successive occupants can also listen without linking it to a reply. As others take their turn at the podium, the very continuation of the procedure — Alexander's means-whereby on a social level — converts the space from a metonym of unquestionable imperative to an ongoing operation, in which declarations of need are subjugated to the constant of agreeing to occupy the space as speakers. Membership is not restricted. Nothing is excluded but the principle of self-reference itself. "The people" ceases to be an idea and instead simply takes place, as a project focused on how to organize sound — how to organize *the air*.

At this point, though, we come up against an interesting antinomy. In the case of the Occupy movement, the grounds of a public thing, the bald fact of a place inhabited by people, can be forced by the indiscriminate acceptance of any petition to speak. With Alexander, on the other hand, we saw that every attempt to speak taxed the procedural mind, such that the successful initiation of a flat practice was most feasible when speech was reduced to a whispered vowel. Saying anything and saying nothing — how might these two practices be reconciled? Is there any intersection between them?

In the context of an individual, speech appears as alien to the implicit mind, because the sequence of utterances follows rules of inference that simply do not exist in its procedural instructions. These rules of inference, after classes are built up into predicates, are confined to temporal sequence. A noun will normally follow the word "of," but there's no specific noun that follows it every time. The declarative mind runs through an inventory of replacements until it chooses a noun on uncertain grounds. The procedural mind, meanwhile, has the motor sequences it has learned through repetition, and while these may serve to blunt the shock of speech to a degree, their applicability to semantics is entirely a matter of rote. How, then, are we to form utterances at all without overpowering instinct?

One obvious way is to relax the rules of inference. Take no thought for what you shall say. This option is consistent with our example of the human microphone. Within the space of its practice, there are no mandatory talking points for any given speaker and therefore no possibility of straying off-topic. *Pace* Badiou, there are only bodies and language — and publicly demonstrating as much forces a truth.

Our only problem here is that we underestimate how persistent the rules of inference really are. To echo our original complaint about OOO (as its canonical form is generally advanced), there is no clear evidence of when we're bending the rules and when we are not. Maybe it isn't explicit enough that the human microphone procedure exceeds some authority. The possibility of a set that does not belong to itself seems to persist, since one of the speakers could actually have the goal of preventing others from speaking — and a filibustering speaker must be admitted along with the others. In fact, in the strictest sense, every speaker does this, insofar as others are kept waiting for their turn.[13]

With the directions, then, we find it difficult to maintain both flatness and word order, while with the human microphone, we meet an obstacle in maintaining both equanimity and *speaker order*. Interestingly enough, when the importance of word order is weakened far enough, the importance of speaker order diminishes as well. There is a point at which the rules of inference become so weak that an utterance by another speaker no longer counts as an interruption. Utterance dissolves into babble, which, to the extent that it's intended as babble, allows for simultaneous utterances.

---

13   At Zucotti Park, preference was actually given to non-white and non-male speakers. Wikipedia, s.v. "human microphone," http://en.wikipedia.org/wiki/Human_microphone (accessed June 30, 2014).

As a matter of formal possibility, then, both the directions and the human microphone could be extended to force the grounds of vocal expression. The idea might not be as ludicrous as it seems at first blush. In the introduction to this inquiry, I compared the practice of object orientation to the ephemeral nature of music, and as it turns out, one outcome of this practice could actually *be* music.

But wait—doesn't music follow rules of inference as well? Well, yes and no. It's true that most cultures have expectations of rhythmic, harmonic, and tonal iteration. ("That's not the *real* Japanese court style," etc.) It's also the case that music, although apparently not about anything at all, is vigorously hijacked to every conceivable end. Rousseau was probably not the first to notice the relation between music and reference when he wrote about melodies that seemed to speak only to their presumed audience.[14] Organized sound is at once both un-possessable and fervently claimed.

Yet there are also traditions in which such claims are actively challenged. The free music movement of the mid-20th century made it its mission to produce sound unencumbered by rules of inference. As of this writing, one can find invitations online to join "ecstatic singing" events — group vocalizations expressly devoid of pre-determined plan.[15] And in any event, one wants to include the vast underworld of impromptu melodic or rhythmic fragments created by people just going about their daily business. That's a form of radiance too. Humans are polymorphously musical.

Our nth task, then, could be to create a public thing that maximizes the possible number of musical participants, while reducing the recourse to reference as far as can be — Rousseau's general assembly expanded indefinitely, with syllabic order and speaker order dissolved.

14 Jean-Jacques Rousseau, *The First and Second Discourses together with the Replies to Critics and Essay on the Origin of Languages,* trans. Victor Gourevitch, ed. Victor Gourevitch (New York: Harper & Row, 1990), 283–84.
15 "Ecstatic Singing Seattle," http://www.meetup.com/Ecstatic-Singing-Seattle/ (accessed June 30, 2014).

Of course, sound isn't the same kind of object as currency or food, and as objects change, so do the challenges. It would do no good, for example, to look for an utterance that remains separate from a recognizable sequence of sounds. There is no absolute sound in this sense. What we're looking for instead is the impulse to vocalize that precedes the machinery of reference, precedes even the choice between speaking and singing, and then a forum that captures that impulse from a maximum number of "vocalists." Let's give this imagined activity the name "*khōra* calling," with a nod to Plato's term for the formless substrate that pervades the universe, and, of course, the clear suggestion of a *chorus*.

What would *khōra* calling entail? How would it take place? I'd be a fool to claim to know the innovations tomorrow will bring, but the technology of today suggests a provisional plan. First, assume an online platform that allows for simultaneous vocal input and output, which users can access anonymously from any device — basically, an online game platform designed to support group vocalization. Then build into this platform an *inverted* speech recognition program. Instead of identifying known words and ruling them in, the program would recognize them and rule them *out,* giving priority to vocal sounds with the least linguistic content. Follow that up with a music recognition program, and invert that too, so as to rule out known musical content as well. These inverted recognition protocols would then drive read-outs of the various singing sessions in progress, with the least referential results appearing at the top of a list on the participant's screens, leaving the participants to hum or jabber or shout as they please.

While one can imagine new referential structures arising within these improvised choruses — codes within the *khōra* — the system would always be vulnerable to the entry of any vocalization whatsoever. Conversely, if participants decided in favor of lots of structure — pronounced rhythms and identifiable words — that too would be their prerogative. The favorites on the list would only be *relatively* free of reference, while those more heavily laden with reference would simply be rotated out of the listings.

No doubt the basic program would need to be tinkered with to meet nuts-and-bolts concerns. How many languages can a recognition program actually filter out? How many vocalists can participate in a single session before it turns to mush?[16] Would it be better to design the audio input so that only a hum comes through? Should there be an option to record? What about video capability?

Khōra calling would also be limited by outside forces. For one thing, the communication lines themselves would not be public. As with a room in which kinesthetics are taught, or a private park in which democracy is exercised, it would survive at the pleasure of an owner somewhere behind the scenes. The possibility would also exist that hackers might try to infiltrate other devices under cover of anonymity. Then, too, people without the right technology might be unable to participate, and people without the best technology could be disadvantaged.

Yet within these constraints, there are positive signs. *Khōra* calling would "happen" on an object one could reliably approach, thereby allowing it to be brought to zero in a methodical way. It would be non-reproducible at any point where reproduction was sought as a means to prop up finality. Moreover, its anonymity would render membership in the pool free for the seeker of social equality *and* the student of the self *and* the patriot, without any conflict between them. Interestingly, the procedure would be largely embedded. Even the prompt to inhibit reference would not appear, as it did with the anonymous mark on currencies. Rather, it would take the form of an automated gatekeeper, letting pass only those impulses that run diagonal across the soundscape of the known.

And that lets the swerve back into the game. To the degree that the *novelty* of these outcries could be reproduced, their es-

---

16 The maximally public scenario — a network of phone users on conference calls — would have to conquer latency, the mouth-to-ear delay of a sound, which varies depending on the medium through which it travels.

cape from our mouths would herald a practice that goes beyond ethics to include aesthetics, a carpentry of the air that belongs to no one, an effect without provenance: the songs of our strange companions.

ACKNOWLEDGMENTS

The Means Whereby a Book...

Any essay that uses the word "existentialism" anywhere in its pages ought to quote Kafka, and I don't plan to miss the party. I will, however, depart from the tradition of invoking his most depressing scenes and instead turn my attention to a certain train bound for the Nature Theatre of Oklahoma, which everyone can join and, from the looks of it, seems to be about nothing at all. Kafka doesn't give us anything to disabuse us of this initial impression. *Amerika* ends, in classic asymptotic fashion, without really ending. The protagonist doesn't arrive, the future lies in wait, the train rolls on.*

The preceding pages have been an exercise in establishing something very like this theater. I began by articulating the problem of coincident entities and, taking it at face value, sought to resolve it in set-theoretic terms. I then showed how these terms could be used to explain a practical method of freeing these entities to behave "independently together." On the strength of this explanation, I went further and incorporated non-human objects into my thesis, and, using the same set-theoretic terms, sought to show how we might encounter objects independently of our idea of them, letting them occupy their own place or ethos through the semi-controllable introduction of monotypical effects. My idea throughout was to locate a formal structure of grounds forcing, which carried its own incompleteness with it and so wouldn't provide a master plan so much as a range of

---

* Franz Kafka. *Amerika*, trans. Willa and Edwin Muir (New York: Schocken Books, 1996).

approaches that could be applied according to how matter, in its untotalizable vastness, presented itself. The results have arguably been less than dramatic, but they are, literally, *almost* about nothing and patently free for anyone to take up.

As for this object that is now a book, I've gone about writing it in a kind of parody of the principles it advances. My model was not the monastic scribe flush with resonant hours, nor the boundary breaker who sacrifices all for art, nor even the dutiful writer for pay. The closest parallel is probably Descartes, who tested his hypotheses in many contexts as he traveled about medieval Europe, except that Descartes sought necessity, and I what lies beyond it. In keeping with that spirit, I tried to treat the act of writing as contingent — while I was actually writing — and then to test those results, not only against other texts, but also against whatever I happened to be doing next.

It's a peculiar way to string sentences together, to submit to the equivalence of "yes" and "no" at every word choice, and not at all the emotional style to which I was accustomed, but after a while, I found I was no longer writing my way out of fear, or into frustration. As more time passed, it also became easier for me to put the writing aside, or even to stop at a moment's notice, without trepidation that I would "lose the thought," since, if I was doing what I was writing about, I would simply be continuing the thought into my tasks at hand. Conversely, if I found myself oblivious to my surroundings while rehearsing a passage, I could be sure that passage was somehow amiss. Gradually, the compositions I reserved for the page came to belong almost anywhere in my day, even as thinking them rearranged my personal assemblage of needs, organizing an inventory of objects and events that did not, in a surprising number of cases, depend on my authorial pride to impress their importance on me.

And so, in the end, this book happened, while costing my part of the world very little. Where I have incurred debts, this epilogue will serve as an acknowledgment of my gratitude: to my editor, Eileen Joy, whose generosity, daring, and commitment to an open-ended process are rare attributes indeed; to Sigrid Hackenberg y Almansa, who not only provided invaluable advice but did so with a warmth and expansiveness that made the revision process a pleasure; to an anonymous critic who scared me straight; to Vincent W.J. van Gerven Oei and Natalia Tuero German, who wonderfully turned my manuscript into a published fact; to my wife, Claudia, with whom I've entered a termless pact that decenters me in ever more breathtaking ways; and to our sons Jonah and Elias, whose radiance — creative, comic and cunning — is undeniable. For those who have chanced upon these words for other reasons, I hope the outcome has at least not contradicted the general case I've made for the defeat of correlationism, not once and for all, but iteratively, out here, where everything is. Of course, since you've already read the whole book, it's a little late for me to ask you to approach it in this light. Rather, then, I ask only that you regard it as yet another contingent thing, to accept or reject, in the astonishing parade of whatever comes next.

Appendix
Greater Than Zero, Less Than Everything

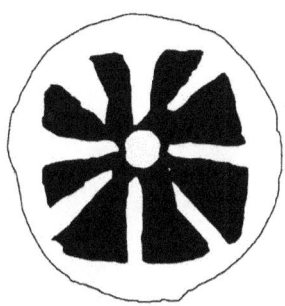

The design shown above lacks any known meaning except for its dim connection to the dawn of coinage. The proto-coin on which this rendering is based (the artist being yours truly, with some commitment to clumsiness) belongs to the so-called geometric electrum series,* discovered in Asia Minor in what was once the city of Miletus, and dates to around the sixth century before the Common Era. But this really tells us very little. The object itself offers only its weight, which follows the Lydo-Milesian standard, a protocol observed throughout much of the region.

The site of its discovery doesn't do much to establish a context, either. Though within the bounds of present-day Turkey, Miletus was part of the Greek colony of Ionia at the time the

---

* "*RJO 47*. Electrum 1/12 stater (1.26 g), about 600–550 BC. *Obverse*: 'collapsing square' with two cross lines. *Reverse*: central pellet with eight radiating spokes." Robert J. O'Hara. "Ancient Greek Coins of Miletus," *rjohara.net*, http://rjohara.net/coins/geometric-electrum (accessed January 28, 2015).

electrum was struck. Yet the Greek case for provenance is also weak, since it could just as well have been produced under the control of neighboring Lydia. And the Lydians have the least say of all because, quite simply, they no longer exist.

The design thus gives us an intention, plain and simple, stripped of its referential raiment. I offer it here not as a direct nomination for forcing the grounds of currency onto itself, but rather to show that such candidates do exist, and can be found, and aren't just the idle fantasies of a would-be philosopher-king.

BIBLIOGRAPHY

Agamben, Giorgio. *Homo Sacer: Sovereign Power and Bare Life*. Translated by Daniel Heller-Roazen. Stanford: Stanford University Press, 1998.

———. *State of Exception*. Translated by Kevin Attell. Chicago: University of Chicago Press, 2008.

Alcoholics Anonymous: The Story of How Many Thousands of Men and Women Have Recovered from Alcoholism. New York: Alcoholics Anonymous World Services, Inc., 2001.

Alexander, F. Matthias. *The Use of the Self: Its Conscious Direction in Relation to Diagnosis, Functioning, and the Control of Reaction*. 3rd ed. Bexley, Kent: Integral Press, 1946.

———. *Constructive Conscious Control of the Individual*. Downey, CA: Centerline Press, 1985.

Althusser, Louis. *On the Reproduction of Capitalism: Ideology and Ideological State Apparatuses*. Translated by G.M. Goshgarian. London/New York: Verso, 2014.

Anscombe, G.E.M. "Modern Moral Philosophy," *Philosophy* 33.124 (1958): 1–16.

Anselm, Saint Archbishop of Canterbury, M.J. Charlesworth, Gaunilo. *St. Anselm's Prosologion*. Oxford: Clarendon Press, 1965.

Aristotle. *Nichomachean Ethics*. Translated by F.H. Peters. New York: Barnes & Noble, 2005.

Badiou, Alain. *Being and Event*. Translated by Oliver Feltham. New York: Continuum, 2005.

Bagaria, Joan. "Set Theory," *The Stanford Encyclopedia of Philosophy* (Winter 2014 Edition), Edited by Edward N. Zalta. http://plato.stanford.edu/archives/win2014/entries/set-theory/.

Bennett, Jane. *Vibrant Matter.* Reviewed by Noel Castree. http://societyandspace.com/?s=Jane++Bennett.

Bergson, Henri. "Introduction to Metaphysics." Translated by T.E. Hulme. *Revue de Metaphysique et de Morale* (1903). http://www.reasoned.org/dir/lit/int-meta.pdf.

Bernstein, N.A. The *Coordination and Regulation of Movements.* Oxford: Pergamon Press, 1967.

Blouin, J.S. et al. "Interaction between Acoustic Startle and Habituated Neck Postural Responses in Seated Subjects," *The Journal of Applied Physiology* 102–4 (April 2007): 1574–86.

Bogost, Ian. www.bogost.com/blog/latour_litanizer.shtml.

———. *Alien Phenomenology, or What It's Like to Be a Thing.* Minneapolis: University of Minnesota Press, 2012.

Bratman, Michael. *Intention, Plans, and Practical Reason.* Cambridge, MA: Harvard University Press, 1987.

Bryant, Levi R. "Three: Strange Mereologies." *Larval Subjects.* May 1, 2010. http://larvalsubjects.wordpress.com/2010/05/01/three-strange-mereologies/.

———. "The Ontic Principle: Outline of an Object-Orient Ontology." In *The Speculative Turn: Materialism and Realism,* edited by Levi Bryant, Nick Srnicek, and Graham Harman. re:press: Melbourne, 2011.

———. *The Democracy of Objects.* Ann Arbor: Open Humanities Press, 2011.

———. "Entropy and Me." *Larval Subjects.* March 5, 2012. http://larvalsubjects.wordpress.com/2012/03/05/entropy-and-me/.

———. "Polymorphously Perverse Nature." *Larval Subjects.* August 17, 2013. http://larvalsubjects.wordpress.com/2013/08/17/polymorphously-perverse-nature/.

Butler, Joseph. T*he Analogy of Religion, Natural and Revealed, to the Constitution and Course of Nature. To Which are Added Two Brief Dissertations. I. Of Personal Identity. II. Of the Nature of Virtue.* Oxford: At the University Press, 1849.

Cantor's Diagonal Argument, A Most Merry and Illustrated Explanation (With a Merry Theorem of Proof Theory Thrown

In). http://www.coopertoons.com/education/diagonal/diagonalargument.html.

Chisholm, Roderick. *Person and Object: A Metaphysical Study*. London: G. Allen & Unwin, 1976.

Clark, Andy and David Chalmers. "The Extended Mind." *Analysis* 58.1 (January 1998): 7–19.

Cohen, Paul. "The Discovery of Forcing." *Rocky Mountain J. Math* 32.4 (2002): 1071–1100. http://projecteuclid.org/euclid.rmjm/1181070010.

Dawkins, Richard. *The Extended Phenotype: The Long Reach of the Gene*. Oxford: Oxford University Press, 1999.

Dennett, Daniel C. *Consciousness Explained*. Boston: Little, Brown and Company, 1991.

Descartes, Rene. *Discourse on Method and The Meditations*. Translated by F.E. Sutcliffe. Harmondsworth, Middlesex, England: Penguin, 1968.

Dewey, John. *The Collected Works of John Dewey*. Edited by Jo Ann Boydston. Carbondale: Southern Illinois University Press, 1967–1991.

Doucleff, Michaeleen. "Dirty Money: A Microbial Jungle Thrives in Your Wallet." *Shots: Health News from* NPR. April 23, 2014. http://www.npr.org/blogs/health/2014/04/23/305890574/dirty-money-a-microbial-jungle-thrives-in-your-wallet.

"Ecstatic Singing Seattle." http://www.meetup.com/Ecstatic-Singing-Seattle/. Freud, Sigmund. *Totem and Taboo: Resemblances Between the Psychic Lives of Savages and Neurotics*. New York: Vintage, 1946.

George, Alexander, and Daniel J. Velleman. *Philosophies of Mathematics*. Malden/Oxford: Blackburn, 2002.

Hamkins, Joel David. "The Set-Theoretic Multiverse: A Model-Theoretic Philosophy of Set Theory," The City University of New York The College of Staten Island of CUNY & The CUNY Graduate Center New York City, Philosophy and Model Theory Conference Paris. June 2–5, 2010, http://lumiere.ens.fr/~dbonnay/files/talks/hamkins.pdf.

——— and Bendikt Lowe. "The Modal Logic of Forcing," *Transactions of the American Mathematical Society* 360.4 (April 2008): 1793–1817.

Harman, Graham. "A Fresh Look at Zuhandenheit." In *Towards Speculative Realism: Essays and Lectures*. Winchester and Washington, DC: Zero Books, 2010.

———. "On Vicarious Causation." *Collapse II*. Edited by Robin Mackay (2007): 187–221.

———. *Quentin Meillassoux: Philosophy in the Making*. Edinburgh: Edinburgh University Press, 2011.

Heidegger, Martin. *Being and Time*. Translated by John McQuarrie and Edward Robinson. New York: Harper & Row, 1962.

———. *The Question Concerning Technology and Other Essays*. Translated by William Lovitt. New York: Harper & Row, 1977.

Hume, David. *A Treatise of Human Nature*. New York: Barnes & Noble, 2005.

Jones, Frank Pierce. *Body Awareness in Action: A Study of the Alexander Technique*. New York: Schocken Books, n.d.

Kafka, Franz. *Amerika*. Translated by Willa and Edwin Muir. New York: Schocken Books, 1996.

Kanamori, Akihiro. "In Praise of Replacement," *The Bulletin of Symbolic Logic* 18.1 (2012): 46–90.

Kant, Immanuel. *Groundwork of the Metaphysic of Morals*. Translated by H.P. Patton. New York: Harper & Row, 1964.

Kierkegaard, Soren. "Repetition, A Venture in Experimenting Psychology (October 16, 1843), by Constantin Constantius," in *The Essential Kierkegaard,* edited by Howard V. Hong and Edna H. Hong. Princeton: Princeton University Press, 2000.

King, Hilary. "Definition: Startle Response." http://www.hilaryking.net/glossary/startle response.html.

Koehler, Evelyne et al. "Hearing Sounds, Understanding Actions: Action Representation in Mirror Neurons." *Science* 297 (2002): 846–48.

Korsgaard, Christine. "Personal Identity and the Unity of Agency: A Kantian Response to Parfit." *Philosophy and Public Affairs* 18.2 (1989): 101–32.

Lacan, Jacques, "The Instance of the Letter in the Unconscious, or Reason Since Freud." In *Écrits: A Selection*, translated by B. Fink. New York and London: W.W. Norton, 2002.

Laclau, Ernesto. *Emancipation(s)*. London: Verso, 2007.

Ledford, Heidi. "Plants Perform Molecular Maths," *Nature News*. June 24, 2013. http://www.nature.com/news/plants-perform-molecular-maths-1.13251.

Leibniz, Gottfried Wilhelm. "A New System of Nature." In *Philosophical essays,* edited by Roger Ariew and Daniel Garber. Indianapolis: Hackett Publishing Company, 1989.

Lewis, David. "Many But Almost One." In *Ontology, Causality, and Mind: Essays on the Philosophy of D.M. Armstrong,* edited by Keith Campbell, John Bacon, and Lloyd Reinhardt. Cambridge: Cambridge University Press (1993): 23–38.

Livingston, Paul. "Agamben, Badiou, and Russell," *Continental Philosophy Review* 42.3 (2009): 297–325.

———. "Realism and the Infinite." *Speculations IV* (2013): 99–107.

Locke, John. *An Essay Concerning Human Understanding*. Edited by Jim Manis. Hazelton, PA: The Electronic Classics Series, Pennsylvania State University-Hazelton. http://www2.hn.psu.edu/faculty/jmanis/locke/humanund.pdf.

Lucretius. *On the Nature of Things*. Translated by Frank O. Copley. New York: W.W. Norton, 1977.

Magnus, Rudolph. "Cameron Prize Lectures on Some Results of Studies in the Physiology of Posture." *The Lancet* 11 (1926): 531–36; 585–88.

Meillassoux, Quentin. *After Finitude: An Essay on the Necessity of Contingency*. Translated by Ray Brassier. London and New York: Continuum, 2009.

———. *Iteration, Reiteration, Repetition: A Speculative Analysis of the Meaningless Sign*. Translated by Robin Mackay. Freie Universität, Berlin (April 20, 2012). https://cdn.shopify.

com/s/files/1/0069/6232/files/Meillassoux_Workshop_Berlin.pdf.

Molière. *The Middle Class Gentleman (Le Bourgeois Gentilhomme)*. Translated by Philip Dwight Jones. http://www.gutenberg.org/files/2992/2992-h/2992-h.htm.

Morton, Timothy. *The Ecological Thought*. Cambridge, MA and London: Harvard University Press, 2010.

Nagel, Thomas. "What Is It Like To Be a Bat?" *The Philosophical Review* 83.4 (October 1974): 435–50.

O'Hara, Robert J. "Ancient Greek Coins of Miletus." *rjohara.net*. http://rjohara.net/coins/geometric-electrum.

Olson, Eric T. "An Argument for Animalism." In *Personal Identity,* edited by R. Martin and J. Barresi. Oxford: Blackwell, 2003. http://www.shef.ac.uk/polopoly_fs/1.101685!/file/animalism.pdf.

Parfit, Derek. *Reasons and Persons*. Oxford: Clarendon Press, 1984.

Rousseau, Jean-Jacques. *The First and Second Discourses together with the Replies to Critics and Essay on the Origin of Languages*. Edited and translated by Victor Gourevitch. New York: Harper & Row, 1990.

Rugani, Rosa, Giorgio Vallortigara, Konstantinos Priftis, Lucia Regolin. "Number-Space Mapping in the Newborn Chick Resembles Humans' Mental Number Line." *Science* 347.6221 (2015): 534–36.

Russell, Bertrand. "Mathematical Logic as Based on the Theory of Types." *American Journal of Mathematics* 30.3 (1908): 222–62.

———. *The Impact of Science on Society*. New York: Simon and Schuster, 1953.

Saussure, Ferdinand de. *Course in General Linguistics*. Edited by Charles Bally et al. Translated by Roy Harris. Chicago and La Salle: Open Court, 1986.

Shoemaker, Sydney. "I. Persons and Their Pasts," *American Philosophical Quarterly* 7.4 (1970): 269–85.

———. "Persons, Animals and Identity," *Synthese* 162.3 (2008): 313–24.

Ting, Lena; J. Lucas McKay. "Neuromechanics of Muscle Synergies for Posture and Movement." *Current Opinion in Neurobiology* 17.6 (2007): 622–28.

Wikipedia. "Human microphone." http://en.wikipedia.org/wiki/Human_microphone.

Wilby, Michael. "Subject, Mode and Content in We-Intentions." *Phenomenology and Mind* (2012. http://philpapers.org/archive/WILSMA-4.pdf.

Wittgenstein, Ludwig. *Tractatus Logico-Philosophicus.* Translated by C.K. Ogden. New York: Barnes & Noble, 2003.

www.ingramcontent.com/pod-product-compliance
Lightning Source LLC
Chambersburg PA
CBHW071700170426
43195CB00039B/2401